livology

Cedar Forge Press

Livology
321 High School Road NE, Suite 253
Bainbridge Island, WA, 98110, United States

Published 2015 by Cedar Forge Press
Printed in the United States of America

19 18 17 16 15 1 2 3 4
ISBN 978-1943290-0-48
Library of Congress Control Number: 2015947846

Cover and Design by Karen Hoey

livology

a global guide to a **deliberate life**

~

written by colleen mariotti
photos by ron mariotti

volume one **europe**

How It All Began

Nearly three years ago, the Mariotti family decided to sell all of their belongings and hit the road. With three young children, ages 5, 8, and 9, they have traveled to 20 countries and counting. The real journey has been in becoming intentionally adventurous parents, students, and observers of the world. This book is a story and an invitation, but beware - once you engage in this journey there is no finish line.

Are you ready to live it? At the end of each story you will find a practice called a "livit." These exercises are designed to facilitate your journey to live more deliberately. They are intended to be there when you need them and do not need to be completed in any particular order. When you feel inspired, open to any practice and watch your day unfold in ways you never expected.

To join the global following and embrace the adventure, visit **www.livology.com**, for inspirational stories designed to help you live more deliberately every day.

Forward

When we first started dreaming of this book, we had trouble thinking of it being something you write in. Originally, it was a coffee table book -to admire and set cups on- shiny, glossy, but distant in a way. We were raised to read and appreciate books but never to write in them. We were taught to take care of books, admire them, and keep them on a shelf alphabetically. Those are good lessons, but they are not the reason for this book.

The fact that engaging with a book in a real and visceral way makes us uncomfortable, means it is exactly the right approach. We know that unease is an exciting sign of personal growth. Our goal with not just our book, but our life, is to engage others to live deliberately from wherever they are in their own journey and that means a different kind of book.

This book is an invitation, but beware – once you engage in the journey, there is no finish line.

We invite you to read our stories and dream of foreign lands.

We invite you to tell your own stories and write your thoughts down. The more you cross out, draw pictures, bookmark, and dog ear, the more this adventure becomes your own. You may even think of highlighting or underlining certain passages when you are going about your day. Open it when you feel like you shouldn't but you must. If you feel like circling, or writing arrows, follow your inspiration.

Perhaps in its most loved moment, it is a book you give as a gift because of what it has meant to you.

This book is organized by seasons as we knew them during our life in the USA, but there is no order to how you move through the stories. The darkest days of winter are the height of summer in some corner of the globe. We encourage you to open the book at random, start from page one, or begin at the end and move backwards. It is important to do what feels good to you. There is no right or wrong way to enter into a more deliberate life.

It is a memoir, travel companion, and journal all in one and it belongs to all of us. It is not our story, or your story, it is collection of dreams that is growing stronger every day.

Are you ready to live it?

Table of Contents

Table of Contents

fall

"If the future is to remain open and free,
we need people who can tolerate the unknown,
who will not need the support of completely worked-out
systems or traditional blueprints from the past."

– Margaret Mead

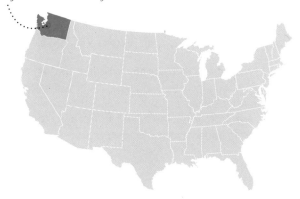

Bainbridge Island, Washington

Are You Tired or Inspired?

We live on a beautiful island surrounded by an azure Sound near an Emerald City, and we are living happily ever after. We are leaving all of it not because we are discontent, but because we are overwhelmingly captivated.

We want to spend more time together in the world with our children while they will have us. We are two teachers who want more than anything to learn what our children have to impart.

We are not seeking greener pastures and bowls full of cherries. Our Island is abundant in both.

We are not seeking cultural festivals and new landscapes to challenge us; we have had beach walks and culinary delights that have shown us undiscovered treasures in our own fields.

We are leaving because we are eager! We are leaving our beautiful Island and our beautiful home. We are selling all of our beautiful stuff, and we are setting out to see the world together.

We are not tired of our life. We are inspired by our life. We hope you enjoy coming on this journey with us, as it is not about travel; it is about growth, and that is what unites us all.

We do not know where this journey will take us. We are leaving all that we know and stepping into uncertainty. We are so excited to see what new islands await us, not because they are better or different from what we have, but because teetering on the edge of comfortable brings us closer to ourselves and each other.

Today I am deliberate about adventure.

- Take an adventure today. A walk through the woods or down a new street, or a drive to a new landscape, will suffice. You could even start a new book if your legs won't carry you down a new path.
- How does it feel to be an adventure-seeker?
- Take this heightened awareness and excitement for the unexpected into your day.

Today I am deliberate about adventure because I know that teetering on the edge of what is comfortable expands my potential in every direction.

"I do believe in simplicity. It is astonishing as well as sad,
how many trivial affairs even the wisest thinks he must attend to in
a day... When the mathematician would solve a difficult problem,
he first frees the equation of all incumbrances, and reduces
it to its simplest terms. So simplify the problem of life,
distinguish the necessary and the real. Probe the
earth to see where your main roots run."

– Henry David Thoreau

Bainbridge Island, Washington

Go Ahead, Sweat the Small Stuff

We started our life on Bainbridge Island in an 800-square-foot cottage with three kids. We were going to build a larger home, but we built a larger family instead; then we were too busy to think about building a house.

The gift of that time together was that it completely changed our relationship to "stuff." My rule was that it had to have a place. If it did not have a place, something had to go to give it a place. It wasn't lack of space for stuff; it was respect for the stuff we said was important enough to have in our lives.

During this past summer, we sold almost everything we owned, preparing to wander the world for a while. We displayed it all nicely, people came and left and all the stuff went with them.

I was stunned at my lack of attachment to things that had so many memories attached: the chair where we had rocked our children to sleep, the collectible dishes that marked their births, and the china we received as wedding gifts, which symbolized our rite of passage into adulthood.

As I told stories to strangers who were leaving with our stuff, I felt lighter. I know that it was not the chair that rocked my babies; it was me. The dishes did not commemorate their births or our wedding; the people who gave them to us did. All of these stories made me feel an overwhelming sense of gratitude for where we have been and the people and experiences that are now giving us the courage to go where we have not been before.

What I learned about the stuff we did not sell is that we need to have enough respect for it to put it away. I realized why I had always had that rule: "a place for everything and everything in its place." Yes, it is important to pick up the toys so I don't step on them, but that is not why everything needs to have a place. The reason is, if you care enough about something to put it away carefully, when you take it out again, you see it in a new light. You appreciate it more than if it lived on the floor or slung over the end of the bed year-round.

When it becomes a burden to rewrap breakables every holiday season, or to put the summer clothes in the attic, listen to that voice that says they don't have a place here anymore. It is when we keep too many things unintentionally that they lose their significance and their splendor. Putting things away, even just the dishes in the cupboard, makes them shine the next morning when we are ready for coffee.

It is not about stuff. It is about home and the things that we surround ourselves with that make us feel loved. Our definition of home is not static, even if we stay in one place. Our stuff needs to keep flowing as well, or there will be a sense of misalignment. The stuff moved on, and I feel like there is more space inside me for this next adventure.

livit

Today I am deliberately sorting those things in my life that add value from those that I no longer need.

- Select one pile, shelf, or corner. Don't open drawers or closets yet, just an area that is out, visible, and needs attention.

- Sort into three piles: To Do, To Purge, and To Store. Only accept a pile you can finish in the time you have today. It is important to finish, even if it is a small stack. If it is something to do, do it! If it is something to purge, purge it! If it is something to store, store it!

- Make sure you see the value in what you are storing, and you are not just keeping something to avoid the emotions that keep you from purging. It needs to add value today to be worth keeping and storing.

Today I am deliberately sorting those things in my life that add value from those that I no longer need in order to create space for inspiration.

notes

A Census on Senses: Celebrate Your Surroundings

I have noticed that in preparing to leave the place I have lived all my life, I am celebrating my surroundings with a renewed sense of appreciation. Perhaps the cream rises to the top when we know it will be the last time for a while. Or perhaps these beautiful treasures have been here all along, and I just got too busy doing to notice.

I want to remember this feeling in each place that we land, so that it is not only in the 11th hour that I am grateful, or only during goodbyes that I savor eccentricities. I want to appreciate each moment of each day that I inhabit a particular place.

Since we have decided to use the world as our classroom and head out for some "long-term slow travel" this fall, I have been thinking about the Pacific Northwest and the beautiful images that will always be with me, having been lucky enough to grow up here, such as:

- Salty, dormant fog
- Earthy cedar groves just after rain
- An Orcas Island hayloft in August with a sweet, overgrown blackberry tang
- Syrupy lupine fields at Mount Rainier that make me feel small and powerful simultaneously
- The rush of the North Fork of the Snoqualmie River when the spring breaks
- The feeling of waiting for ferry boats to arrive, only to have time completely suspended once on board
- The audible burst I can hear when the sun shines, followed by soulful basking
- The nesting rain and how it centers everything

- The sweetness of wild mountain blueberries mashed together with huckleberries and a dash of honey
- A cloak of emerald green that is loyal year-round, if I just look up
- The way my feet sink into the moss floor of the National Forest in March and I feel safe and protected
- The contrast of an Orca whale against the ultramarine sound
- The blue of the cracked robin's egg in the seagull's beak

This is home. I am sorry for not appreciating it more all along, but I promise to take the beauty of the place with me, and to arrive open to appreciating the splendor in each new place with a renewed sense of wonder and tenacity.

Today I deliberately notice the natural beauty that surrounds me.

- From where you stand right now, what beauty do you notice?

- Set your watch for one minute, and just observe the view from the window or the yard.

- Intentionally put yourself in a natural setting, on a patch of grass if that is all you can find, and spend one minute focused on the nature that you see.

Today I deliberately notice the natural beauty that surrounds me because that connection energizes me and changes who I am in the world.

notes

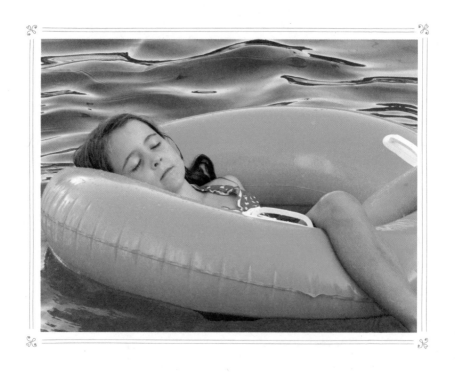

"Dear Naps,
I'm sorry I was so mean to you in Kindergarten."

– Author unknown

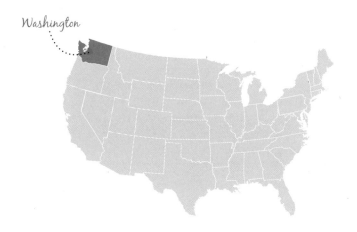

Washington

Do You Have the Courage to Take a Nap?

What does inspiration feel like? Last June, as I thought about the kids getting out of school for the summer, all I wanted to do was take a nap. I think of taking a nap daily, mind you, but I have not succumbed since the day after Christmas.

Somewhere in my well-conditioned brain, it feels like an accomplishment to ignore that voice. Am I not stronger if I do what I am supposed to do, not greedily following what my heart desires? I sometimes feel the need to justify following that little voice. *I must work hard before I am deserving.* I tell myself, *Things have been so busy, and I have not slept in days, months, years!*

The key to all joy and fulfillment lies in listening to that voice. My voice did not emerge to be ignored. It is waiting for me to remember what my kids know so well. Follow it, and you will feel unbridled joy. The voice did not just start, and it is not going away. It is the inspiration that is inside me. It is my personal GPS, and yet I rarely follow it. Why? Because I was taught, by others who were not following their own hearts, that it is selfish or irresponsible.

Inspired action can be scary because it comes from the deepest parts of who we are, and it often does not align with what others think we should be doing or what we believe, out of some sense of guilt, we should be doing. I have found that when I have the courage to listen, whether it is a desire to take a nap or a desire to take my family of five on a wandering journey across the globe with no definite ending, it is the only way to live. The alternative means I am living someone else's idea of life.

Nap time starts now!

livit

Today I deliberately pay attention to my own inspiration by acknowledging it when it arises.

- Today is about listening to your own ideas that bubble from within.

- Without looking back with regret or forward with rigorous goals, simply commit to jotting down your own inspired thoughts when you have them today.

- You don't need to take any action beyond acknowledging that voice inside. The results will astound you.

Today I deliberately pay attention to my own inspiration by acknowledging it when it arises because I know that when I listen to my own voice, my actions align with my dreams.

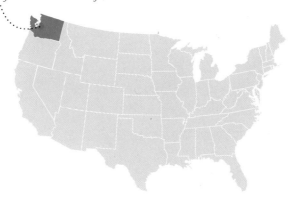

Bainbridge Island, Washington

Have You Ever Thought of Running Away?

"If you run away, you take yourself with you." I heard these words a hundred times growing up. It was sound advice, but still I ran. I ran to Australia as an exchange student, and I spent a year a hemisphere away from my family at the age of 15. I ran to the former Soviet Union with a performing group and witnessed Chernobyl. I ran to China for an economic history tour during the Handover. I ran and ran and ran, and although I was excited about travel, I was also running from something.

I am older now, and I feel differently. Running away has an air of fear or weakness attached.

Maybe it is not running away at all. Maybe it is running to ...

I am not running away from tradition;
I am running toward creativity.

I am not running away from making a first impression;
I am running toward being more present.

I am not running away from over-scheduling;
I am running toward intention.

I am not running away from play-dates;
I am running toward gaiety.

I am not running away from corporate politics;
I am running toward global awareness.

I am not running away from convention;
I am running toward ingenuity.

I am not running away from networking;
I am running toward uniting.

One is not possible without the other.

Toward is not better than from, as one gives birth to the other, if we are willing to see the beauty in the contrast. I always come back profoundly changed.

You do not need to travel to see the contrast, but if you do travel, you have to work hard not to see it.

Today I deliberately move in the direction of my dreams by shifting my thoughts to running toward something I want, versus away from something I don't want.

- Think of one aspect of your current life that you would like to change. What is the new reality you are hoping to create in this situation? Be specific.

- Next time you are accused of running away, focus on what you are running toward and hold that image.

Today I deliberately move in the direction of my dreams by shifting my thoughts to running toward something I want, versus away from something I don't want, because I know that change is inevitable when my vision is clear.

notes

"There are far, far better things ahead
than any we leave behind."

– C. S. Lewis

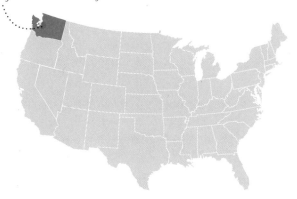

Looking up Through Rose-Colored Glasses

When I was in elementary school, every morning at 6 AM, I would sleepily wander from my bed to the front porch to check the weather for the day. Some days it was eminently clear what the day would bring. The splash of the rain on my toes confirmed the patter that invaded my dreams the night before. There were also those rare summer days in the Pacific Northwest where you know it is going to be perfect from the second the sun comes up. No fog needs to lift or mist needs to clear. The day has dawned, and it smells of blackberries and sweet hay.

There were other days when it wasn't as clear. I would stand there as the air washed over me and feel the day. Sometimes I could smell rain, see a pewter snow cloud in the distance, or feel a marine mist settling in. I would watch the cedars and pines rustle but hold tight to their goods to maintain our Evergreen State reputation. I would slowly wake up with the day and see what it had to tell me, long before I spoke a word to anyone.

23

Now, I often look down at my phone instead of through the window to check the weather. I often trust my GPS even when it doesn't feel right versus stopping to ask for directions. Sometimes I text neighbors to ask for a cup of sugar instead of just walking over to say hello. Times have changed ...

Perhaps it is a romantic notion to think of moving away from smart technology in an effort to "connect" with each other more. We want our kids to be wise in the ways of technology just as they are in other subjects, but we do not want to look down anymore.

We are leaving on this journey with one laptop, no data plan, and no handheld entertainment devices. We will watch TV in other languages, scour local libraries for books in English, and ask for directions in our best attempts at local languages. We will lean on each other and at times on total strangers to help us navigate the world. I get a little teary thinking about turning in my smart phone, but the truth is, just because it makes my life easier, I am certain it is not making me smarter. I was much more resourceful and courageous before we met.

Pie in the sky? Maybe, but the excitement I feel just thinking about it, discomfort and all, lets me know it is exactly the right thing to do.

Here's to looking up through rose-colored glasses!

Today I deliberately look from a place of appreciation at the people and places that surround me.

- Make a commitment to leave your phone behind for just one stop today. Whether it is getting coffee, picking the kids up at school, or grabbing lunch. Make sure your phone or tablet is not accessible or audible.

- Connect with people. Just be in the space you inhabit. Listen to the sounds, take a deep breath, and appreciate what you experience.

- Notice any discomfort you feel while looking up, and know that feeling is vulnerability. It takes courage to be present, and you will be rewarded.

Today I deliberately look from a place of appreciation at the people and places that surround me, because I know that each moment I have the courage to be present is a moment I will never forget.

notes

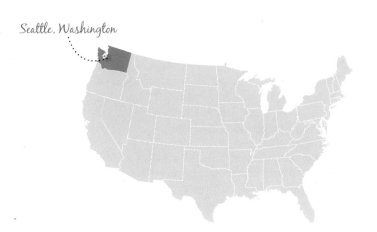

Seattle, Washington

Spreading Your Wings

I finally understand what is meant by "Life is not about the destination, but the journey." It almost sounded cliché to me until I began this journey around the globe with eight and ten-year-old boys. Even when the destination is knowingly Disneyland and I am trying to describe all my favorite rides, they are completely focused on taking flight:

- While I am judging how the car we hired to drive us to the airport could possibly cost $100, they are entranced by the neon lights that line the floor of what was, in 1989, the latest and greatest stretch limo.

- While I am rushing to security to make sure we have enough time to unpack all of our liquids, empty our pockets, and remove five pairs of shoes, they are fascinated by the X-ray machine—so much so that the TSA operator gives them little wings and lets them hold the wand for a moment.

- Because I am so good at being really early, we now have two hours to wait at our gate before our flight. My mind is racing with educational activities we could engage in to fill up the time. When I look up, the boys are mesmerized by the planes taking off and landing. They are asking each other questions like, "What do you think makes a soft landing or a bumpy landing? How do they keep the planes from crashing into each other when there are no lines in the sky? Do you think pilots like to travel as much as we do?"

- Finally, we are on the plane. All the adults are requesting and fighting over aisle seats so they have a quick way off, and the kids are crawling over each other to the window seats so they don't miss a moment of the journey!

- I take a huge breath and get snacks and games organized for the flight. I overhear the boys trying to guess who will be the lucky person who will get to sit with them in their row. Their enthusiasm wins over even the weary business traveler who has won this special seat. Soon this lucky lady is offering them gum and showing them pictures of her pets as they engage in adult conversation with grace, humor, and joy.

- Just when I am thinking of how much coach services have shrunk in recent years, the boys let out a little yelp of joy: "The cart is coming! The cart is coming!" They put their trays down carefully, so as to not make "no soda" eye contact with me, and they order ginger ale and peanuts. Because they used their best manners, the flight attendant gives them the can of soda and peanuts and cookies. They truly cannot believe they are being showered with such abundance!

I have arrived. I am forever changed. Entranced, fascinated, mesmerized, momentous, enthusiastically abundant. That is my new definition of travel!

livit

Today I am deliberate in my gratitude for everyday activities that I may take for granted at times.

Try any one of these things today:

- When your children come into the room, look right at them in greeting and really see them with joy.

- On your drive to work, notice how well your car functions and how comfortable it is, and make note of any natural beauty on your route.

- When you eat anything, take a moment to say thanks for the fuel, and really try to taste and experience the food.

- As you move through your day, notice the ways in which your body serves you. Give thanks for your breath, your feet that carry you up the stairs, your hands that can be held, your eyes that take it all in.

- Find any and every way to simply notice what IS working today.

Today I am deliberate in my gratitude for everyday activities that I may take for granted at times because I know that the more I see what IS working, more of those things will come into my experience.

notes

"I am not waiting. I am not waiting for anyone any more.
It was me I was waiting for."

– Priya Parmar, *Vanessa and Her Sister*

Anaheim, California

What Is Your Happy Place?

In early September, during our visit to Disneyland with my parents, we were all sitting on the train that goes around the park. I was feeling nostalgic as the conductor yelled, "ALL aboard," and closed the gate. This was the last time we would be with my parents for a while, and it was a dream come true to be in Disneyland with our children and their grandparents.

Just as the tranquility washed over me, a woman came running up to the gate after it had closed and yelled at the conductor that she needed to get onto the train to get to the parade in time. She was visibly upset, huffing and puffing and disturbing the peace! How could she ruin my moment? And then I realized she can't. This is the happiest place on earth.

It was clear, looking at this very unhappy woman, that I was happy by choice. I also did not need to leave my happy place to join her in her discomfort. Just because she was unhappy in my happy place, I did not have to leave. She did not have the power to steal this moment, unless I gave it away.

I was happy, sitting there, in spite of the 100-degree-plus temperatures, the endless lines, and the grown men in Goofy hats with Yoda backpacks. I am happy because I choose to be, in any given moment!

It is powerful to think that no matter where I am and what I am facing, I can make a choice to be happy or not. This woman also believed that she would be much happier if she could just get to her destination. I can relate to that trap. There are so many moments in a day when I think, If I just get through this meeting, or finish prepping this meal, or planning this party, then I will be happy.

It is never true. There is never a happy ending to an unhappy journey. Even if the train has left the station and I am still on the platform, I am surrounded by possibility. All of it begins with my courage to choose happiness over resistance of any kind. All aboard!

Today I deliberately choose happiness over resistance.

Think of one IF/THEN in your life today:

- IF I lose this weight, THEN I will buy that outfit.
- IF I make this much money, THEN I will take a vacation.
- IF I finish this project, THEN I will go for a walk.

Pick one IF/THEN that exists for you, and rewrite it into a positive, present-tense affirmation using AND.

- I am good at taking care of myself, AND I appreciate nice clothing.
- I find joy in my job every day, AND the rewards are infinite.
- Projects give me a sense of accomplishment AND productivity.

Release the IF/THEN, and affirm the AND. Get ready for your new, improved reality.

Today I deliberately choose happiness over resistance because I recognize it is a choice, no matter what external factors swirl.

notes

"Nothing is more difficult, and therefore more precious,
than to be able to decide."

– Napoléon Bonaparte

New York, New York

What Is Citizenship?

I have never thought of myself as the best American. From a very young age, I took every opportunity I could to travel overseas, and I never tired of being away—the farther, the better.

When traveling in Mexico, I would cringe when Americans would raise their voices, thinking that would help the Mexican people understand English more clearly. I learned how to say, "I don't speak French," in Swedish while on our honeymoon, so the Parisians would not know I was American. I was not a proud American because I didn't understand what it meant to be an American, until very recently.

The inspiration for leaving on this journey at this time was born from an opportunity to apply for dual Italian-American citizenship. Once we discovered that we could give our kids citizenship to the 27 countries that make up the European Union, as well as their United States citizenship, we were already one foot out the door, as any "less-than-enthusiastic" American would be! Little did I know, this process of dual citizenship would ignite in me an intense appreciation for what it means to be American.

We decided to visit my husband's family on the East Coast on our way to Italy. It has always been a dream of mine to show our kids the Statue of Liberty and Ellis Island. I wanted to show them where their relatives first entered this country and what it meant to them to become American, but the truth is, I didn't know myself.

As we boarded the ferry toward Liberty Island and approached "The Beautiful Lady," as she is often named, I started to cry. There was a recording on the audio tour: "The definition of liberty is the condition of being free from restriction or control; the right and power to act, believe, or express oneself in a manner of one's own choosing." I know this idea of liberty meant something very different to our ancestors who immigrated, but the concept of liberty, with its inherent accountability and risk, washed over me. I was overcome, 100 years later, for very different reasons. The audio tour continued, "Her right foot is raised, as if she is continually on the move, facing the Old World and beckoning people to the New, the fire in her torch symbolizing knowledge and light."

As the tears continued to fall, I realized we were exercising the same liberty offered to new Americans, to become more informed citizens of the world. Had our ancestors not risked their lives to get to America, had we not been born with this entitled sense of freedom, I am certain we would not be able to dream as big as we have to make leaving on this journey possible.

I am so grateful to be a United States citizen because it has given me the unalienable right to life, liberty, and the pursuit of happiness. I will do my best to represent our country with the humility and grace it deserves, as we go back toward the Old World, leaving the New behind, at least for now.

Today I deliberately exercise my unalienable right to life, liberty, and the pursuit of happiness.

- Think of a time in your life you felt freedom. What contributed to that feeling? What were the circumstances surrounding your freedom? Most importantly, how did that freedom feel, and how would you describe yourself during that time?

- If you have ever felt it, it is within you, and you are capable of that feeling in this very moment without any further action plan. Just take that feeling into your day.

Today I am deliberately exercising my unalienable right to life, liberty and the pursuit of happiness because I know that any time I experience a lack of freedom, regardless of my environment, I have the power to feel differently.

notes

"Keep me away from the wisdom which does not cry,
the philosophy which does not laugh, and the greatness
which does not bow before children."

– Khalil Gibran

London England

Kids Only: No Entry Unless Accompanied by a Child

On our recent trip to London, we came across a park that was massive and fully gated, right in the middle of the city. After walking around and around, trying to find a way in, we found the gate. The sign read, "Welcome to Coram's Field Park. Adults May Only Enter if Accompanied by a Child." What a cute gesture, I thought to myself. It turned out it was not a sweet sign but a serious message. "No entry to over-16's Unless Accompanied by a Child." How did I know they meant business?

My husband and I decided to get a workout early one morning while the kids played at the park. During the time we were not by the kids' side, not one, not two, but three adults who work on the grounds approached us to let us know this was not a place for unaccompanied grown-ups. We had to wave to our children and call out their names before the staff would leave us be. I was stunned, and the kids were thrilled! They had never felt so welcome!

Captain Thomas Coram was a philanthropist who opened the first orphanage in London in the mid-1700s. The park pays homage to his work and, to this day, is in alignment with his vision. The park was a special place. Even the bathrooms were just for girls and boys. The sinks were low, the toilets were lower, and the floors were shined. I thought of how amazing it would be if more places celebrated kids in this way. To our surprise, we found London to be a city made for children.

The British Museum had a family desk with themed scavenger-hunt booklets that led the kids on wild chases through history. The games led them purposefully up and down the many floors of what would have been a very overwhelming museum. The National Science Museum had an entire floor dedicated to kids: hands-on experiments complete with shows on the hour about structures or explosives. The best part was National Museums are free for everyone!

Sunday we decided to explore the Royal Parks for a taste of family time in London. At Regent's Park there was a kids-only paddle-boat lake, complete with mini-boats and a deserted island to explore. We even spotted a group of teenagers playing quidditch! The boys could not believe their eyes. We headed to Hyde Park for the afternoon to have tea and play in Princess Diana's Memorial Playground, complete with a security gate and buzzer and a pirate ship to rival Jack Sparrow's.

Thank you, London, for bowing to my children. They are forever changed by your act of honoring them!

Today I will deliberately honor all children.

- Everyone has different opinions about children, how they should be raised and what they should eat, because every one of us knows what it is like to be a child.

- Today make a commitment to honor all children, your own if you have them, without judgement. Practice seeing them for who they are, observing their joy or pain, and celebrating their ability to be so connected.

Today I will deliberately honor all children because I know the more accepted and celebrated they feel for who they are, the more clarity they will have about who they hope to become.

notes

Rome, Italy

When in Rome ...

After being in Italy for fewer than three weeks, I believe we have picked the perfect country to teach us about slow travel in all the right ways. The discomfort that comes from leaving our American pace behind has been palatable. For example:

- I decided to have my hair done in Rome. After three hours, as I was still in the chair and people all around me were smoking, laughing, and drinking espresso, I felt forgotten. I felt my "I am the CUSTOMER" speech lurching in my throat, but somehow I knew the moment should be observed. *When in Rome*, I kept telling myself. *When in Rome*. I left after four long hours, loving my hair and feeling proud that I had swallowed all that I knew, long enough to just let it happen.

- I realized shortly after our arrival in Italy that clothes-dryers were almost nonexistent. Not only that, but when you start a load in a small, Italian washing machine, the cycle takes 2–3 hours. Then you hang the clothes to dry, often inside, with no central heating (until after Oct. 15th, I am told) to dry them, and presto: they are dry two days later. As a mother of three, I can tell you, this has been a challenge. Last night, however, as I was tucking my son in, he said, "My sheets never smelled this much like home at home." There is something to be said for slow laundry!

- As I have learned repeatedly while running errands with the kids, almost everything, in almost every city, even H&M in Rome, closes from 1 to 4 or maybe 5, for lunch. After the initial inconvenience of it all, I asked the one person I found who spoke English why everything was closed. She told me that lunchtime in Italy is sacred. Many kids get out of school at 1:00 or 1:30, and everyone meets at home for their main meal of the day. She believes it is the reason the familial structure is still more intact in Italy than in some other countries. It is worth noting that the divorce rate in Italy is only 12%, as compared to close to 60% in the United States. Now when I see *chiuso* signs for three hours in the middle of the day, I smile, imagine everyone enjoying family time, and remember that is the reason we are on this journey.

- After the towns, villages, and cities wake up from their mid-day *riposo*, it is time for *passeggiata. Passeggiata* is a slow, gentle stroll through the main streets of the old town or *centro storico*. This also means that very few restaurants are open for what we call dinnertime in the United States. Most restaurants do not even open their doors until 7 PM, and because our children are famished by then, we are usually the only people sitting down to eat before 8 PM. Again, slow travel is a choice, and *passegiata* is the perfect metaphor for slow travel. No one is in a rush to get to their destination. Some have dressed up, many arm in arm, meeting, greeting, hugging, kissing, and walking. The purpose is to connect. Even if it means we are waiting by the door for the *pizzeria* to open, it is worth every moment.

Italy, even in its busiest cities, has mastered the art of a graceful pace. We are still clumsy and stumbling and at times resisting, but we can feel the peace artfully washing over us.

livit

Today I am deliberate in my efforts to move more slowly during times that matter.

- Pick one interaction you have planned for today, whether it be lunch with a friend, dinner with the kids, or a coffee break.

- Commit to not watching the clock, answering the phone, or multi-tasking just for this one interaction.

- Afterwards, take note of the quality of the interaction and the fulfillment that only comes from authentic connections.

Today I am deliberate in my efforts to move more slowly during times that matter because establishing a genuine connection with others makes me stronger and healthier.

notes

"I haven't been everywhere, but it's on my list."

– Susan Sontag

Molise, Italy

To Be or Not to Be: Are You an Uber-Planner?

I have learned how to play Magic the Gathering, Monsuno, and Ms. Mary Mack in the last 30 days. I have had my hair and make-up done by my five-year-old daughter countless times, and my boys have made me several custom airplanes, complete with our newly designed family crest. I have many friends at home that were really good at doing all the above-mentioned activities and then some, but I was not. I was the uber-planner. I was always one step ahead, packing lunches, laying out clothes, planning social engagements, cooking for family parties, pre-writing and filing birthday cards so they would not be forgotten.

I woke up today, 50 days into our adventure, and I was looking up homeschool trackers, planning menus, and asking my husband about his contact-management forecast and our plan for the holidays. I heard a dull thumping in my head that after hours turned into a loud roar: *BASTA* (enough in Italian)! This is why I am here, now. This is not about orchestrating; it is about listening to the music within that I am used to quieting while I "get stuff done!"

Today is about doing what I am inspired to do. When it feels scary and vulnerable to listen to my inspiration, my uber-planner rears its ugly head. Why? Because that was my defining self at home. I was so good at planning, organizing, and creating space for people to gather—even if it meant barking at the people who matter most not to mess anything up! It is not that efforts to always be prepared were wrong, but they did not bring me joy. I was addicted to being ready, which meant I was unable to be present. Here, I couldn't prepare for tomorrow if I wanted to, because the grocery store is a like a riddle, the spreadsheets are in a foreign language, and navigating takes teamwork.

Now things are messier, spreadsheet-free, and impulsive, and that is exactly the discomfort I want to feel. I know on the other side of this discomfort is a presence like I have never felt. I know this because I hear the kids' laughter when I am on the floor, playing. I see their relief when we get up to go find gelato and we leave the game just as it was. They know I am coming back to play some more.

Ready or not, here I come!

Today I am deliberately playful and present.

- What is something on your list today that requires preparation? Does it excite you to think about preparing, or does it feel draining?

- What are some alternatives to the preparation, if the task doesn't excite you, that would allow you to be more present?

    Can you delegate some of the preparation?

    Can you cancel the engagement?

    Can you order out or contract the work?

- Be honest with yourself. Sometimes we think we must do things in order for them to get done correctly as a defense mechanism that keeps us from the honesty of the present moment.

Today I am deliberately playful and present because today will only come once, and I want to savor it.

Positano, Italy

Attempting to Communicate the Meaning of Amalfi

I will never forget how I felt the day after our wedding. I remember people were trying to show me photographs they had taken and share stories from the day, and I just wanted to hold it silently in my heart for a second longer. It was as if words and pictures would somehow color my memories, and I just wanted to fully develop them in my mind before I saw them through the experience of others. I had a similar impulse on our trip to the Amalfi Coast last week. I could not look down for a moment to write anything, and if I did, words were insufficient to describe the experience.

We were quiet on our way home from our five-day trip. It was as if we were developing each frame in our own memories before attempting to communicate what the time meant to us individually. Eventually, after looking at the photos over the weekend and sharing things that stood out for each of us, our stories became a collection, but our recollections were our own.

We visited Sorrento, Amalfi, and Ravello, and we fell in love with Positano. It is a harrowing drive with a snaking highway and a sun-bleached town that is stacked between endless cliffs. It was not love at first sight. There were over 800 aging, crumbling steps between our apartment and the beach. Streets stopped and started without warning, and directional arrows were only sometimes accurate. The beaches were rocky and the locals well-versed in American pricing, and we were head over heels in love! Positano lured us in, one majestic moment at a time. Once we arrived at the bottom of the 800 steps, the water was no longer a murky ceylon but a lapis blue. Looking up, the cliffs seemed to touch the clouds as they magnified the seagulls' cry and roosters' chorus. The pebbles tumbling in the tide were beach-chair lullabies for the most reluctant sun-worshippers.

At sunset, Positano was truly radiant. The lights came on slowly and lazily as the antique street lamps cast a buttery glow over the cobblestones. It looked like every calendar cover I have ever seen of Italy, and yet it was impossible to believe that it was real. Just when I thought it could not get any more serene, the burning apple wood perfumed the air, and the hibiscus that had basked in the sunlight all day was luminescent.

I still feel as though words are not sufficient to describe such a place. I am so grateful for experiences that stun me into silence; places where looking down at a book or a blog would be a betrayal of the beauty that calls for a sacred sort of quiet.

Today I am deliberate in seeking the kind of beauty that stuns me into silence.

- Feast your eyes on one thing today that is so beautiful it silences the world around you. It may be a landscape, a dew-laden spider web, or the red cheeks of your child coming in from outdoors.

- Let the beauty settle around you and just say, "Thank you."

Today I am deliberate in seeking the kind of beauty that stuns me into silence because the beauty I see is equivalent to my ability to appreciate it.

notes

"It's easy to understand why the most beautiful poems about England in the spring were written by poets living in Italy at the time."

– Philip Dunne

Capri, Italy

Capitalizing on Lessons from Capri

I can't even count how many times I was told, "Don't waste your time with Capri; it's not worth it. There are TOO many tourists." Over and over again, I heard the naysayers, but I could not get the romantic notion of this island out of my soul.

Since we were on the Amalfi Coast for my husband's birthday, the kids and I decided, if the weather held, we would take him to Capri. On October 25th, when the tourist season had virtually ended the previous week, we woke to 80-degree temperatures. This was our chance! It was surreal when our Audrey Hepburn-style picnic boat picked us up for our seven-hour tour of the Isle of Capri. I was still hearing the naysayers' whispers, although our family represented the largest group of tourists in sight. All doubt dissipated as Capri came into focus. The sun-soaked cobblestone streets had an antique parched aroma that is so true to Italy. The lemons dropped from the trees and peppered the rooftops. The saccharine bougainvillea seemed to disappear into the cliffs and reappear near the sea. The grottos and arches were like precious gems in a regal crown.

What I learned the moment Capri came into view was that there is a reason tourists flock from all over the world to come here. Sure, I would have loved to come here before all the designer shops took over the hillside. I would have loved to see the pure, virgin beauty of this place that the Emperor Tiberius deemed it worthy as a vacation spot from AD 14 through AD 37. It would have been magical to see the Capri that gave people like Thomas Mann or Pablo Neruda inspiration. The island defies all normal parameters of beautiful.

I agree with the naysayers in that I would not have had the experience I had on Capri during high season, but it is the most beautiful place I have seen on Earth to date. Going off-season allowed me to experience it in all its splendor. The beach we hiked to would have been private just weeks before, but it opened up during the off-season. Many of the restaurants were closed, but the *salumerias* and fruit stands were overflowing with fall's harvest. On the picnic boat home, our host provided us with *prosecco* and lemon tarts. As we cruised along the Amalfi Coast back to Positano, my son asked a quiet question: "Does it get any better than this?"

I learned it is just as much about time as it is about place. More importantly, acting in the direction of your dreams, even when others feel your time would be better spent elsewhere, is critical.

Today I deliberately trust my own voice.

- Decide right now that you will trust your own decisions today. When you feel unsure or the need to seek permission or approval, take a deep breath, and follow your inner guidance system.

Today I deliberately trust my own voice when others share their opinions about my thoughts and actions because I am the expert on me.

notes

"Any arbitrary turning along the way and I would be elsewhere;
I would be different."

– Frances Mayes, *Under the Tuscan Sun*

Cortona, Italy

Rediscovering Your Holiday Spirit

When we started having children, a dear friend began giving us beautiful Christmas Village houses every year to collect and some-day pass on to the children. Every year, as we would unpack the village, one building at a time, we would imagine what it would be like to live in such a place. We would place the ceramic characters carefully, connect the cobblestone paths, and talk about what the crunch of the snow sounded like on Christmas Eve. When it was set up perfectly, we would turn out the lights, and the amber glow would pour from the windows and lanterns, casting an ethereal radiance on our season.

As we prepared for this journey, there was no room for the Christmas Village in our suitcases. We talked about how we would have to come up with some new traditions while we were away. As we drove up the winding Tuscan lane to the little and stately hilltop village of Cortona, the kids exclaimed, "It looks exactly like our

Christmas Village! We are going to live in our Christmas Village!"
We were all beside ourselves as we explored and found our favorite Christmas Village businesses, complete with the butcher, the
baker, and the candlestick maker.

Cortona is astonishing. It is bathed in fiery Tuscan light and rooted
in generations of Italian families with a generous mix of monks,
students, and expats to keep things bustling. There is a fine air in
the perfectly presented shops, but there is no pretense. There are
famous works of art in very accessible, yet proud, museums and
piazzas that have pulse, rain or shine. The movies *Life is Beautiful*
and *Under the Tuscan Sun* were filmed in Cortona.

Although Cortona has every reason to be touristy in its offerings,
it has remained artisan and grounded. Fewer than 2,000 people
live within the partially Etruscan walls, which date back to the 4th
Century BC. The Cortonese love to say: *"Cortona è la mamma di
Troia e la nonna di Roma."* That is, "Cortona is the mother of Troy
and the grandmother of Rome."

So far, we have been in thirteen churches in Cortona. Some of
them have ancient foundations from pagan temples that support
awe-inspiring examples of Renaissance or Byzantine architecture. Although the architecture varies dramatically, there is one
constant when we stand before these many churches. When we
are lucky enough to be near a church as the bells begin to swing,
we can hear them rocking in an ancient dance, and they prepare
to sing. For just a moment, after the bells toll, the rocking can be
heard again, until stillness overcomes them.

As our footsteps crunch along a pea gravel path and we watch
the sunset over the Tuscan valley and hill towns, we know we have
imagined our way right inside our own *piccolo villaggio di natale.*

livit

Today I am deliberate about choosing the people and things that surround me this holiday season.

- As you prepare for the holidays, think about your ideal season. What does it look like, feel like, sound like? Is it full of festive parties and friends? Is it a time to connect with your immediate family by the fire? Is it a time of healing or celebrating?

- Spend five minutes today, thinking "selfishly" about what you want out of this season of giving. This vision will help you as you field invitations from family, coworkers, and friends, and it will give you a framework for how to respond and move through this time of year.

Today I am deliberate about choosing the people and things that surround me this holiday season because I know if I have the courage to hold my vision, the new year will find me restored and ready.

notes

*"Start by doing what is necessary,
then what is possible, and suddenly
you are doing the impossible."*

– St. Francis of Assisi

Tuscany, Italy

It Is Not About What You Should Do

My husband and I have had countless conversations about organized religion and have been to numerous services at different churches since we met. After we had kids, we spent a lot time trying to find the right place for our family, to no avail. We kept it light with the kids, as we tried different services and Sunday Schools, and we kept quietly searching.

As soon as we stopped searching, it happened. A gratitude ritual evolved naturally, no formal sermon required. In the past two months, without saying a word, the kids have begun moving toward churches no matter where we are. They sense the splendor in the architecture, the joy in the bells, the awe in kneeling at the pew. Completely of their own volition, they enter churches, pick their own pew, and close their eyes. When they are done, they get up and quietly explore the side chapels and crypts, even using their own euros to light candles for different reasons. We haven't studied Roman Catholicism or done units on Renaissance or Byzantine architecture. The kids have a reverence that can only come from within.

Last week, as the temperature dropped and the rain set in, I announced that we were going on a hike to a monastery. This news was not well received, but I persisted. We walked from Cortona, to Le Celle, which is where Saint Francis retreated for reflection and solitude. His "celle" is still completely intact, and there are friars living true to his ways to date. We walked on the same blustery wooded path as Saint Francis until we reached Eremo Le Celle (1211), whitewashed on the verdant hillside.

The kids were stunned into silence as the waterfalls rushed down the mountain, bursting with autumnal rain. It seemed so natural to us to connect with the sacred spaces of the Patron Saint of Animals and Ecology. Saint Francis was said to have practiced his sermons to woodland animals during his visits to Le Celle. We sought refuge from the storm in pilgrims' chapels along the path, listened to the chickens clucking and the bells tolling, which spoke of the friars that we never laid eyes on but knew were present. Our five-year-old proclaimed, "I bet they are somewhere warm, counting their blessings."

Our hike through the Tuscan hills to Le Celle inspired us to venture to Assisi in Umbria the following day. Assisi was bathed in sun, and the Basilica of San Francesco d'Assisi was the kids' favorite church so far in Italy. While visiting the crypt of Saint Francis, many people were moved to tears. People of many faiths were present and brought to their knees as they descended into the beauty of the crypt from the upper church ordained by the famous frescoes of Cimabue, Giotto, and others. We wandered into the San Francesco woodland that wound down into the valley for a few miles below Assisi. We had the privilege of seeing the ruins of the 13th-century monastery of Santa Croce, which was once inhabited by Benedictine nuns who treated weary pilgrims.

We all decided that our pilgrimage in the rain to Le Celle was the closest we have ever felt to so many things.

Today I deliberately give thanks in whatever way feels most natural to me.

- You have probably heard many versions of, "Be grateful," or, "Give thanks," throughout your life. Today is not about what you "should" do. Today is about who you are and how gratitude flows from you naturally.

- One of the best ways to reflect on this for yourself is to pay attention to what you appreciate in others. Do you notice when someone holds a door open for you or lets you merge on the freeway? Do you notice someone's warm smile every day? Do you hear kindness when someone is talking to their children?

- Today just pay attention to what you notice in others, and you will come into giving effortlessly.

Today I deliberately give thanks in whatever way feels most natural to me because, although there are many ways to give thanks, feeling thankful is where the magic happens.

notes

winter

Siena, Italy

Aspiring to Be Offline and Connected

We visited a police station last week as part of our residency verification process for the citizenship applications. After walking past all 10 offices and the front lobby, there was not a computer or cell phone in sight. It was the first time in ages we remember seeing notepads, pens, crusty coffee cups, and newspapers taking up desk space. If the officers needed something, they hollered, sauntered, or whistled from room to room. No email, texting, or tweeting in this establishment.

I thought maybe it was a little pocket of tradition until I learned otherwise. I finally found Wi-Fi on a street corner in Siena, and having been offline for days, I was eagerly checking in with family and friends when a lovely woman approached me and asked me, *"Ti sei perso?"* ("Are you lost?"), while pointing at my phone. I realized after looking around that I was alone in my screen fascination. Teenagers were walking arm in arm, eating gelato, children were playing a lively game of soccer, couples were drinking wine, and families were getting market goods for dinner. It was an amazing, bright Sunday afternoon in Piazza del Campo, and I could not see another human with a screen.

Technology is here. It has a place in this culture, but it is not at the table in a restaurant or at a café with friends. It does not have a place in the *piazza*, where people meet to spend time together, and it is not invited to the weekly market. Relying on technology here would mean relying on people less, and that is not a sacrifice most Italians are willing to make.

Today I am deliberate in my use of technology.

- Think about when you may use technology to escape being present.

- Make a conscious effort today to leave your phone off or in the car when you are entering into an interaction or environment where you may rely on it unnecessarily.

- See how your experience transforms as you look up at people and places with new focus and attention.

Today I am deliberate in my use of technology because I know that true connection comes from being present with people who are part of my experience now.

notes

Italy

Family-Friendly Italians

Everywhere we have gone in Italy, without exception, our children, and all children, have been not just welcomed but enveloped! Store owners come out of shops to grab their cheeks and give them oranges and *dolce*.

- The man who makes stationery with a 100-year-old letter-press, grabs their hands and leads them into his workshop to pick out a special card or handmade journal.

- The servers squat down and listen to the kids' attempt to place their order in Italian. Inevitably, the server cheers, *"Brava!"* or, *"Bravo!"* with an encouraging, joyful air when the kids are finished ordering.

- We spend a lot of time in parks here, or running errands, just as we did at home. We are both humbled by how the Italians, in general, talk to their children. It is not as though kids are indulged in a negative way. They are listened to, heard, and enjoyed by not just their own family but also their community.

- When our children have been somewhere they are not supposed to be, or doing something they are not supposed to
  do, they have been redirected by complete strangers in loving ways that enhance their understanding of this culture
  and how to be successful here.

It is truly amazing that we have not encountered any punitive
commands from anyone in this entire country after 12 weeks of
traveling. Our time has been full of misunderstandings and cultural blunders. Instead of lectures, we have been assisted by people
who truly want us to be successful. Hotel employees have offered
to take the kids into the kitchen and show them how to make
biscotti, while we have a quiet cup of coffee. When our kids have
accidentally broken beautiful vases, or bicycles, they have been
met with people who want to help them. Strangers get their own
hands dirty helping the kids fix things, not because stuff is broken
but because our kids feel badly, and people want them to feel
better.

I am learning so much about how to be with my children differently. I am learning that it is not just acceptable for them to be
children; it is expected, celebrated, and powerful. I have asked, for
the last time in Italy, "Is this establishment family-friendly?" Every
time I ask, people look at me like I am crazy, and they reply, "Of
course!" Then they look at the kids; grab their cheeks, and say,
"Ciao, Ragazzi!"

Today I am deliberately indulging my youthful exuberance.

- What is one of your best childhood memories? A time you felt safe, happy, and indulged, like the world was your oyster?

- Take 15 minutes today to indulge yourself. It could involve buying a special something, tasting a delectable treat, lying on the couch while listening to music, or playing your favorite game.

- Just give yourself the gift of some element of your whimsical childhood memory today.

Today I am deliberately indulging my youthful exuberance because I know the more fun I have today, the younger and freer I will feel.

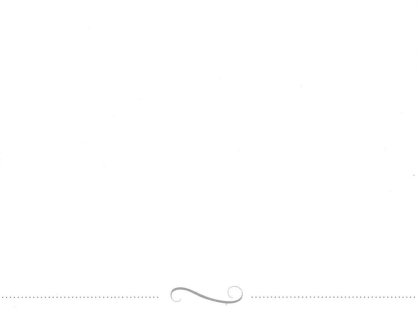

notes

Italy

Is Your Food Market-Fresh?

Eating local is a way of life in Italy. There is no "locavore" movement. It is a state of being. The biggest shift for me, coming from the United States, was the lack of choice. Coming from Bainbridge Island, we felt many similarities at the farmers' markets with access to farm-fresh produce, meats, and cheeses. The biggest difference was that if I wanted something that was not in season at home, I could get it. Luau-themed birthday in January? No problem. Turkey gobbler sandwich during a late-night pregnancy craving in July? Sure! What I give up in Italy are options. What I gain is the most mouth-watering in-season ingredients I have ever tasted.

Each town has a weekly market where most villagers do their shopping. There are some large grocery stores where people buy soap, boxed pasta, and canned goods but rarely meat, produce, or bread. Food is one of Italy's main exports, which means that a large portion of the food consumed in Italy is made in Italy.

The *Parmigiano Reggiano*, which is exported all over the world, has been produced basically the same way for nine centuries! The quality, attention to process, and lack of chemicals in production result in incredible flavor and shorter shelf life. Italians, for the most part, shop small and often. In my hunt for salad dressing at a larger store, a local friend said, "Why would you want to put anything but new olive oil on a perfect tomato?"

At the market last week in Cortona, my daughter stopped in her tracks. When I asked her what she was doing, she replied, "Can you smell that celery? Really, you have to smell the celery!" Eating here is truly an experience.

I feel like I can taste things such as tomatoes, celery, pork, and beef, for the first time. The flavors hardly resemble those I thought I knew. Slow food, yes. Locavore, yes. Organic, yes. Farm fresh, yes. Farm to table, yes. *Buon Appetito!*

Today I am deliberate about the quality of food I purchase and consume.

- Even if today is not a grocery day, think about paring down ingredients and enjoying the simplicity of whole flavors that you already have in the house.

- Make a commitment to eat one snack or meal that consists only of ingredients your grandmother would recognize as food.

Today I am deliberate about the quality of food I purchase and consume because I know the food I consume is a part of me and how it was grown or produced affects me, my family, and future generations.

notes

"Listening is being able to be changed
by the other person."

– Alan Alda

Basilicata Region, Italy

Do You Know the Whole Story?

When I was talking to my parents on the phone, describing a day we spent in a knife maker's workshop a few weeks ago, my dad said, "You know, your great-uncle was a blacksmith, and he used to fabricate things for us out of wrought iron over coal heat." I was stunned for a moment. I always thought of myself as a good listener, and I always spent whatever I time could with my family, young and old. I had never missed holiday gatherings (until this year), birthdays, or graduations. How did I miss this story? How many other stories did I miss while running around productively, with my planner tucked under my arm? I spent an entire day learning about a man in the mountains of Southern Italy and his trade, and somehow I didn't know about how my great-uncle spent his days before he retired.

I have noticed a dramatic difference in the storytelling we are exposed to when we are moving at a tourism pace versus living somewhere new. While traveling in Capri, Rome, Florence, and London, for a week or two at a time, I was told the "brochure" story. It was all I had time for and all I could digest in the time I was investing. You know the story. It is the Hawaiian luau story, which is beautiful and educational, and superficial to some extent, in its packaging. It is truly all I ever wanted to take in during my seven precious vacation days. It is not that these stories were void of learning, but they were far from complete. I loved the stories in more touristy areas because they came to me. I did not have to work that hard; they were colorfully practiced, animated, and served with appetizers. When we moved recently to the Basilicata region of Italy, I was frustrated. What is the story here? I don't get it. There is no brochure!

Living in a home in Southern Italy, nowhere near a tourist desti-nation, we spend our time shopping, chopping wood, walking, and going to produce markets. As we attempt to mail things at the post office, the story of this place is slowly revealing itself. It is not in a brochure, and since I speak limited Italian, I have to really listen, watch, taste, and piece together the richness of where we are currently living. The magical part is in the going to the story, versus having the story come to me. The understanding is much deeper. The flavors are much more authentic because there is no *menu touristico*. The picture is more complete because we are a part of the story.

Perhaps when I was at home, I did not work hard enough to go get the story because I thought it would always be there, and that is never the case. People pass on, and their stories go with them. It is never too late to listen differently ... and to get the whole story.

Today I am a deliberate listener.

- Call or spend time reaching out to one person to-day who has a story to tell that you may not have had time to listen to in the past. You don't need to force it, but you do need to give yourself whatever time it takes to listen.

- Know that it will be productive time in ways you cannot even imagine.

Today I am a deliberate listener because I know that every story becomes a part of me and therefore deepens my experience.

notes

Basilicata Region, Italy

Are Your Lists Controlling Your Life?

I have had the same "holiday list" for 10 years. On my list was everything from Santa pictures to holiday card photo sessions to ordering and shipping gifts—teacher gifts, clients gifts, special homemade gifts—and more.

There was a moment this week when I missed my list and I panicked. When I was executing the list in years past, I was often complaining about how I wanted time to enjoy the holidays, to bake cookies and sit by the fire with a mug of hot chocolate.

This week I had the time to do all the things the list didn't allow for, and I was pining for my list! There is comfort in routine. There is comfort in being home for the holidays. But I couldn't have felt further from home.

I had two choices. I could either replicate the chaos of holidays past, busying myself with a similar list, or I could lean into the space, feel grateful for its presence and see what emerged.

I bought a puzzle! I have never even considered doing a puzzle that was not for my children. I bought a real, 2000-piece puzzle with a lovely scene from Venice. The last two days, when my To Do's of days gone by would have been at their pinnacle, I positioned myself around my puzzle, with tea and lemony *panettone*, and I chatted with my children. I have learned so much about them around the puzzle table. They have told me stories about schoolyard skirmishes and books they hope to read, dreams they have about countries they hope to visit, and tales of holidays past.

Because we have no routine here, and the traditions are so foreign to us, we have the space to dream together. Because of the discomfort, we dream big! If we can do the holidays here, where else might we go? "Let's Google the North Pole for Christmas. I wonder what that would be like." "Oh! Lapland, Finland, looks magical; maybe we will go there next year!" And the conversation is blazing around the puzzle table warmed by the wood stove, full of firewood my husband chopped, with walnuts drying on the mantle, all because we opened ourselves to the possibility of time and quiet in December.

We won't be with our extended families this year, and there will be significantly fewer presents under the tree. But we will be with each other in a way we never have before, and that is the only thing on my "list" this year.

Today I am deliberate about creating space to connect with people who matter the most in my life.

- Right now, write down one way you can spend meaningful time with someone who matters to-day! Is it a phone call, a note, a letter, a lunch date?

- The anticipation of this connection is just the beginning of the rewards that will follow.

Today I am deliberate about creating space to connect with people who matter the most in my life because I know that the real gifts I receive this season are the stolen moments with people I love.

notes

Maratea, Italy

Creating Your Own Soundtrack

I can not walk past a blackberry bush dripping with berries and not pick them. I see jam and cobblers and vanilla ice cream smothered in blackberry sauce, and something inside me says, "Pick." The men in my family are the same way during fishing season. My dad and uncles are always a little on edge if the salmon are running and they are not out on the water, trying to catch them, sunup to sundown.

Although freshly picked apples and mountain trout were attractive and pulled us toward them with tenacity, we all knew at some level that we were not living off the land. I knew that if my applesauce didn't last through the winter, I could get more at a grocery store, or if the fish evaded the fishermen, hook, line, and sinker, a replacement could be purchased.

We are now living in the Southern Apennines. Our first day here, living in the foothills of Massif Sirino, tucked between the Tyrrhenian Sea and a compact series of high peaks, we heard the hunters' shots echo between the cliffs. The bells tied around the

herded cattle in the valley below grew in resonance as they sauntered past the house. The sheepherder's horn calling his flock
just before sunset was the final proclamation that hunting and
gathering and living off the land is something I have never truly
experienced.

At the Saturday produce market, otherwise calm ladies elbowed
and positioned themselves to get the last of the season's spinach
and lemons. At the local butcher shop there were whole rabbits
and wild boar for roasting. Three-wheeled scooter trucks called
Apes (Ah-pees) peppered the country roads, as their masters
scoured the hillsides for firewood, mushrooms and wild greens.
My kids were feverishly gathering walnuts before the rain settled
in because there is no flavor that compares to a fresh, earthy, sun-
warmed walnut.

These are the sounds of the season. I am sure each season has
its own cacophony. It is funny how sounds that seemed so dis-
cordant on day one feel more like a beckoning after a month.
Perhaps it is because I understand them more, or maybe it is the
mystery of a foreign land that is still so enchanting.

**Today I am deliberately aware of the sounds of the
season that bring me joy.**

- Pay attention to sounds today that bring you joy. Is
  it your child laughing, rain on the roof, coffee in the
  morning or the crunch of snow under your boots?

- You are creating the soundtrack so leave out he
  notes that don't resonate for you.

- Write a list of five to ten tracks and turn your
  attention to those today.

**Today I am deliberately aware of the sounds of the
season that bring me joy because I know that what I
turn my attention to I hear with more frequency.**

notes

"Be clearly aware of the stars and infinity on high.
Then life seems almost enchanted after all."

– Vincent Van Gough

Sicily, Italy

New Perspectives on Old Traditions

We arrived on the island of Sicily on January 6th. Epiphany is a national holiday in Italy, and everything is closed. After making our way to a small mountain village called Petralia Soprana, we checked into our bed-and-breakfast only to learn that the only restaurant in the village was closed for the week. Having been on the road for over four months now, our boys said, "Well, there must be a reason. Let's go explore!"

We were drawn to the arresting hill town of Gangi. The village caressed the hillside and illuminated the night sky, beckoning weary travelers to attempt the ascent into the main *piazza*. There was a gentle mist that became fierce as we parked the car and climbed into the pedestrian-only village square. We heard laughing and singing, and it motivated us to keep climbing. We were recompensed with the festival of *La Befana*.

Italian kids look forward to the arrival of *Babbo Natale* on Christmas Eve. Santa Claus, however, is a modern tradition that pales in comparison to the anticipation generated by the arrival of an old witch in early January. *La Befana* comes from Christian legend rather than popular culture. The story states that the Three Wise Men asked the lonely witch to lead them to the stable where the baby Jesus lay in a manger. *La Befana* declined their offer. Very soon she realized that she had made a huge mistake. She quickly gathered up a bag full of gifts and set off alone in search of the baby Jesus. Though she followed the same star as the Magi, she never found the stable. Tenacious as she is, La Befana continues to travel the world over to this day, searching every house for baby Jesus. She leaves treats and small toys for the nice and candy coal for the naughty.

As we stood in this ancient town of Gangi, Sicily, and listened to the village kids sing the *La Befana* song, we were overwhelmed with gratitude for the freedom to learn by doing. The kids quenched their hunger by scrambling with the local children to find candy *La Befana* pitched from the zip line above.

As we crowded into cafés for molten cups of chocolate after the celebration, we felt strangely connected even though nothing was familiar. We celebrated Epiphany in every sense of the word.

Today I am deliberately looking at the traditions of this season and new year with a fresh perspective.

- This new year is less about resolution and more about intention. Inherent in resolutions is a belief that something you have always done needs to change. Resolutions often prove ineffective and short-lived.

- Intention, however, is full of hope, joy, and dreams because, rather than setting your mind to something, you are engaging your heart.

- An example of a resolution transformed into an intention may be: "This year I am going to exercise three days a week," OR, "It is my intention to give thanks every day for my physical body and to do whatever I can do honor my health and well-being."

Today I am deliberately looking at the traditions of this season and new year with a fresh perspective because the acceptance and joy I feel today inspires and strengthens my intentional life.

notes

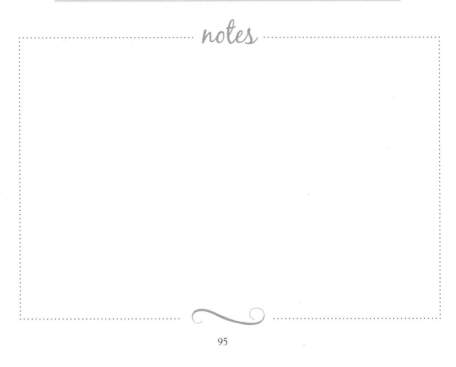

Sicily, Italy

Are You an Adventure-Seeker?

Over the last 10 years, I can remember so many conversations with adventurous friends and family returning from various vacations. People would describe trekking adventures, heli-skiing vistas, and rainforest zip lines, and I would smile and nod and feel tired upon leaving the conversation. I often wondered what was wrong with me. Why is it that all I can imagine doing on a vacation is beaching myself and shutting out the world by diving into a great novel? I wanted to sit down. I wanted to take a shower without being interrupted, and I wanted to eat a meal someone else had prepared. I never once thought about river-rafting through a canyon, until now . . .

Sicily is the largest and most populous island in the Mediterranean Sea. I expected a lot of things from Sicily more in line with overzealous fish merchants and scenes from *The Godfather* movies. I was not prepared for the diverse and natural landscape that opened up before me. The volcanic valleys are lush and Irish green; the mountains are snow-capped this time of year and covered in towering Sicilian fir trees. The orange groves blanket the interior and seem to drop into the sea. We knew we needed to see the towns and cities, but our trip would not be complete without experiencing the natural artistry of this famed island.

We were ready for some family adventure. Parco Avventura in the Madonie mountains of Sicily was surrounded by hundreds of kilometers of nature trails that wound all the way to the sea. We contacted the park owner, and even though the park was closed in January, they planned a day of endangerment just for us! Our guide led us through three-story ropes courses weaving the forest canopy. Our son said all he could hear were the "birds singing and mom screaming!" We spent the remainder of the dappled sunlit afternoon honing our archery skills and completing family orienteering challenges. We all pushed ourselves further than we thought we could go, but the difference was, we did it together.

The adventure was exciting to me because I had energy to spare. I was not running on empty, needing to get away. I felt fulfilled, rested, and joyful when we left for Sicily. I am now seeking new ways for us to grow and challenge ourselves as a family. The stamina to have that desire makes this the greatest ride of my life.

(livit)

Today I am deliberate about planning an adventure I have always wanted to embark on.

- What is your dream trip or experience? Is it a spa down the street, an African safari, or a visit to see a loved one?

- Set a timer for two minutes and give yourself this time so your mind does not wander. Your focus in these two minutes is not to figure out how to make this experience come true—only to picture yourself as if you are already there.

- What does it feel like, smell like, sound like? Two minutes is all you need today!

Today I am deliberate about planning an adventure I have always wanted to embark on because I know the more I am able to imagine, the more likely I am to experience.

notes

"Street food in Palermo is deadly serious."

– Anthony Bourdain

Sicily, Italy

Street to Table: How Daring is Your Palette?

We have tried many different angles when approaching history through travel with the kids. Sicily is certainly not alone in Europe with its vast, rich, and layered history of conquests. We knew to really understand the complexities of the largest region in Italy, we would need a filter to help us digest the antiquity and navigate the current culture. We discussed as a family what we all love to do in Italy, and eat was at the top of the list. It just so happens that Palermo, Sicily, is one of the top 10 street-food cities in the world.

After a full day on the beaches in Cefalu, we headed to Palermo at dusk. The people at Palermo Street Food customized a tour for us that changed the way we see the world. They are volunteers who want travelers to understand Sicily by breaking down stereotypes of Sicilian culture through the most tactile travel experience we have had to date.

Our guide met us in front of the Teatro Massimo (Opera House scene from *The Godfather* movies) at 5:30 PM, and our culinary journey through the strategic crossroads of Europe began. He explained how Sicily is not a melting pot where many people come together to coexist at one time. Sicily, instead, is a trove of thousands of years of history and the architecture, infrastructure, and food of the many ruling cultures. As we wandered the ancient streets, he showed us places where the Arabian hydraulic systems are still in place and functioning today. We followed up that stroll with saffron-laced *arancini* balls, which the Arabs brought to Sicily during their nearly 200 years of rule, beginning in the 9th century.

We sampled *pane con panella* (chickpea fritters) and *croquettes* (potato fritters) that were brightly finished with Sicilian lemon as we paced the dark streets of Palermo. Our guide spoke of the collective legacy of the Phoenicians, Greeks, Romans, Arabs, Normans, French, Germans, Spanish, Italians, and even the British as we tasted our way through history. Our kids were brave enough to eat a *pane cà muesa* (a cow spleen, tongue, and lung sandwich)!

The tour finished with a sweetness we never could have imagined. The grand finale was scoops of *gelato* smashed into a *brioche* bun almost too big to handle. Apparently it is the Sicilians' idea of a perfect summer breakfast! The following day, we wound our way to the resort town of Taormina to try some of the best *cannoli* in the world. It was made with ricotta from goats' milk only and stuffed into fresh, crisp shells while we waited.

As we crossed the Strait of Messina on the way back to mainland Italy, the waves rocked us into silence as we chewed on the memories of the past week. The people of Sicily believe they are Sicilian first and Italian second, but what we will remember most are the colorful individuals who graciously brought this island to life before our eyes.

Today I deliberately try one thing I have never tasted just to spice things up.

- The beauty of a new year is that you have never been here in this new year before. Open yourself to the newness today by simply trying one completely new flavor.

- It may be a flavor in your coffee, a new fruit or vegetable that you don't recognize, or a restaurant from a foreign land that has always piqued your curiosity. It may be as simple as green tea instead of black.

- Whatever it is, let it be easy and fun and slightly exciting.

Today I deliberately try one thing I have never tasted just to spice things up because I know the more I expand, even my palate, the more open-minded I become.

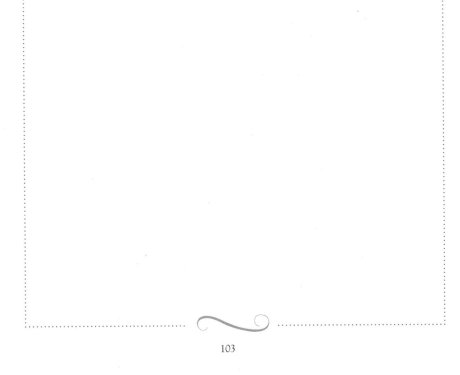

notes

Italy

A Systems Approach: Do You Value Quality or Quantity?

It would be naïve to say that there are no systems in Italy. It would be more accurate to say there are few systems I understand in Italy. It took me three weeks to mail a package to my sister. I visited four different post offices in four villages and gave up after an hour each time.

A neighbor recently told me that when the wait got consistently too long in the town post office, they added a coffee and biscotti service instead of more post office employees. In all my post office attempts, I was the only one visibly in a hurry and visibly frustrated by the "lack" of systems. Of course there was a system; I just couldn't crack the code.

The man at the window kept beckoning his friends who came in hours after me. There was a number system, but it didn't seem to hold a candle to "who you know." I remember looking around during my final attempt and seeing people laughing, drinking coffee, talking, and lounging, and I just wanted to scream, "HOW DO YOU MAIL A PACKAGE?"

Thankfully, my husband was up for the challenge. He decided to be first in line, before the post office even opened, to eliminate the number-machine variable. The only way to do that is to be number one! Even so, it was about relationships. The postmaster wanted to understand who he was, where he was living, what was he sending, why was he in Italy, when he was leaving, and how he felt about Italy so far. He was not interrogating my husband at all. He genuinely wanted to know, understand, and relate! Guess what? He and my husband are now on a first-name basis. If Ron walks in, he is beckoned to the window because he took the time to crack the code.

The beauty about the difference in Italy's systems versus many of the systems in place in the U.S. is that because they are based on relationships, the interactions are personal and meaningful. The kids received ski lessons with Fabio as their big Christmas present. We tried to email, to call, and to check the internet for ski school information. All of those things would have given us the information we needed in the United States. Here, we got in the car, drove to the mountain, and waited for someone who looked like a Fabio to ski down the hill. We then proceeded to attempt to communicate in our limited Italian and set up a time for the kids' first lesson.

The result? Fabio is completely invested in the kids. He treats them to hot chocolate in the lodge and knows how to tease them lovingly, all in a foreign language. The men in the rental shop rub our daughter's cheeks and help her tie her shoes after she turns in her ski boots. The staff behind the Nutella crêpe operation call the kids back if they can't see over the counter and proceed to pile powdered sugar and *dolce* on top of their crêpes until the kids' smiles warm their chapped cheeks.

The systems here seem to lack efficiency based on U.S. standards, but Italians don't care about U.S. standards. Based on my limited knowledge, the criterion for success in Italy is about the quality of the interaction, not the speed with which you are moved through. It is much harder to measure the value of human interaction, but it is something you can't help but feel when you are in this remarkable country. Italy is my slow-travel sage.

Today I deliberately choose quality over quantity.

- When you feel that impatient urge to rush today, stop yourself. Try to appreciate the process and the result that comes from slowing down.

- Pay attention to what you hear and see and how you feel.

- It is important to release any resistance in order to genuinely appreciate quality when speed and efficiency are part of the American way of life for many.

Today I deliberately choose quality over quantity, and I act according to that value.

notes

"I wanted movement and not a calm course of existence.
I wanted excitement and danger and the chance
to sacrifice myself for love."

– Leo Tolstoy

Italy

Do You Believe You Can Have It All?

I have lived a life of prerequisites. It was a game I played in my head every second of every day for many different reasons.

- I can have a cup of coffee after I finish prepping dinner, doing laundry, and paying these three bills.

- Only after I work out can I have that chocolate-dipped macaroon that has been calling my name.

- After I finish my graduate degree, I will take some time off.

- After all three kids are in school all day, I will take time for myself.

Now I live a life of AND's. The only thing that has changed is my ability to believe that I can have it all, now. In the Sicilian dialect, there is no future tense. It took me a while to really grasp this concept, since I was always projecting my life into the future to explain the current sacrifices, or thinking of joys that I had earned at some point in the past through my strenuous effort.

There are many critics who look at the downsides of the Italian culture in their present-tense, *la dolce vita* lifestyle. I am here to soak it in because I had the fast-track memorized with every fiber of my being: education, job, house, family, retirement. I still have all of those things, although no one here really cares where I went to college or what my future plans hold. I don't have to pass an invisible finish line before I reward myself or others. I know I have changed because, although I am still doing the laundry, cooking the meals, and cleaning the various houses we inhabit, we are traveling the world as we go about these daily activities. They have a new life, a new interest, a new allure.

This was the first journey I have ever embarked on where I skipped the prerequisites. We went from dream to reality in four months. Why? Because the vision was clear, and not living in the direction of this dream was not an option. As we blaze this new trail, fresh AND's reveal themselves:

- We can work AND travel;

- We can be active and healthy AND spend time together as a family;

- We can explore the world AND stay connected to those closest to us;

- We can educate ourselves AND our children;

- We can dream AND shape our reality in the direction of those dreams.

It is important to be open to receiving all this journey has in store for us every day. The either/or's are clearly a fear-based defense mechanism that have no place in the land of NOW!

(livit)

Today I deliberately rewrite the either/or's in my life.

- What is one either/or, if/then statement you use regularly?

- If I go to the gym, then I will treat myself. Either I spend time with husband OR my kids. Simply rewrite it as an AND statement, and read it three times. How does it feel to have it all?

- It is just an act of faith. Try it out for today.

Today I deliberately rewrite the either/or's in my life in order to shift my belief into one of having it all.

notes

Mount Sirino, Italy

How to Create the Time You Desire

I have heard and stated so often, "Time flies when you are having fun." I used to believe it until we left on this journey.

I have a whole new perspective on time. Time no longer rules my kingdom because I have an abundance of it. Because I have an abundance of time, I fill it with things I have always wanted to do. Because my time is full of things I have always wanted to do, each day feels like a lifetime fulfilled. Because each day feels like a lifetime fulfilled, these past five months feel like years, decades, lifetimes!

A long day used to have a negative connotation; now it means more time to live a dream. It is not as if time has stopped. It is more as if it has lost its power over me. I took the reins, and all of sudden, I have more of what I once lacked. What was once precious now takes its orders from me. Time is on my side.

We now look at time in relationship to sunrise, sunset, coffee time, tea time, quiet time, and time for a new adventure. Our time in Southern Italy is wrapping up because we have decided it is time.

As Albert Einstein said, "The only reason for time is so that everything doesn't happen at once."

Today I am deliberate in my relationship to time.

- Write a list of three words that capture your average daily relationship with time. If your list falls into the "not enough time in a day" category, write three things you would do if you had the time you believe you lack.

- Pick one thing from your list, and schedule it into your day. Be aware of your relationship with time, and when an expression of lack surfaces, meet it with, "Time is on my side, and I am exactly where I need to be in this moment."

Today I am deliberate in my relationship to time because I know the amount of time I have or don't have is my creation.

notes

Malta

Where Do You Stand?

As the dead of winter wreathed Italy, we turned our gaze farther south. As my husband was coming back from a work errand a few weeks ago, he excitedly shared that he had seen an advertisement for flights to Malta for 20 dollars. We all stared at him blankly before someone piped up, "Where is Malta?" In a few short hours, we were booked for the following week.

A million years ago, Malta was attached to Sicily geographically. We assumed that because it was only an hour flight from Bari, Italy, it would feel very much like Italy. The beauty of Europe is that we were completely mistaken. An hour flight in Europe takes you to a completely different world.

The official languages in Malta are Maltese and English. It felt so luxurious to order meals and purchase books in English for the first time in months. Even though we had the ease of the English language, we had the experience of the Maltese culture. Malta, like many parts of the Mediterranean, has a rich history of conquests, and the Island is papered with layers of contributors, including Greeks, Romans, Normans, Arabs, French, and British.

Malta has the oldest freestanding structures on Earth. These Megalithic marvels antedate the Egyptian pyramids and Stonehenge by 1000 years! Even with this antiquity, Malta feels like a country in its adolescence. Malta has only been independent since 1964 and a member of the European Union since 2003. With a population of 430,000 inhabitants, there is a tangible feeling of history, but also a burgeoning energy that is palatable.

The capital city of Valetta is one of the most beautiful cities I have ever seen. The European Union funds have turned an already statuesque port-side jewel into an international destination for super-yachts and trade moguls. Valetta from the sea is truly something to behold. It was the first time our whole family has gasped simultaneously. Just 30 minutes away, we found ourselves hiking limestone cliffs flocked by Maltese (peregrine) falcons diving into the seemingly endless Mediterranean Sea. The quaint fishing villages with brightly colored wooden vessels riddled the protected crystalline bays.

As we flew away from Malta, the contrast between the lapis-blue water and the washed-limestone infrastructure left an imprint on our souls. It is a country that feels very hopeful, vibrant, and comfortable. How lucky are we to have experienced a place so intimately that we could not accurately locate on a map just two weeks ago?

Today I am deliberate about my knowledge of geography.

- Think about a place you have always wanted to visit. Look at it on a map, and find out how long the drive or flight is from where you stand in this moment.

- What towns or countries border this desirable destination? Take your knowledge of your relationship to this place into your day.

Today I am deliberate about my knowledge of geography because I know that the more I can orient myself in the world, the more likely I am to test what is comfortable.

notes

"Alice! A childish story take,
And with a gentile hand
Lay it where Childhood dreams are twined
In memory's mystic band,
Like pilgrim's withered wreath of flowers
Pluck'd in a far off land."

– Lewis Carroll

Malta

I Yam What I Yam: Dreaming for Real

I will never forget my 10th birthday. As one of four siblings, my birthday celebrations were usually family affairs, but not number 10! I remember vividly my parents telling me I could invite three friends to the movies. I was beside myself. I decided we would go see *Popeye*, a musical starring Robin Williams. As I sat in the theater, feeling like a princess with my popcorn, soda, friends, and family, the matinée commenced.

I will never forget the enchanting set from the movie. I said to my 10-year-old self, "Someday I will see Sweethaven Village." At the time, I did not know it was literal. I think the big screen and the images it brought into my life have always inspired new desires in me. That day in the theater came thundering back to me one day in Malta, as our bus driver said, "Now passing Popeye's Village, the set and scene from the 1980 film *Popeye*." What did he say? It can't be. I scrambled over people as the double-decker bus driver came over the loudspeaker to tell me to sit down. Nothing was going to obstruct my view. There it was. It was truly more beautiful than I could have imagined.

Nestled in a grotto-filled, crystal-clear bay, the fully preserved movie set hugged the coast. It was not the set that gave me the chills but the idea that I set this idea in motion, in a daydream during my 10th birthday party. Like a mirage, it was right in front of me. The waves crashed over the bulkhead as "Popeye the Sailor Man" blared from the speakers, and I feverishly instructed my family that we were getting off the bus.

Once we were on solid ground, I had a moment to really appreciate how powerful childhood dreams are and how incredible it is to want something and then to detach from it and trust it will come in time. I did not know at 10 years old where the movie was filmed, or what about it made me want to go there, but I know for certain that I did not arrive at that place by accident.

Those are the moments that give me the strength to keep dreaming.

Today I deliberately reflect on a childhood dream of mine.

- Think about one thing you dreamed about as a child that has manifested in your life. It was most likely something you visualized and then detached from, trusting your vision enough not to manage it.

- Give thanks for that dream and its presence in your life.

Today I deliberately reflect on a childhood dream of mine because I know the more I acknowledge dreams coming true, the more come true.

notes

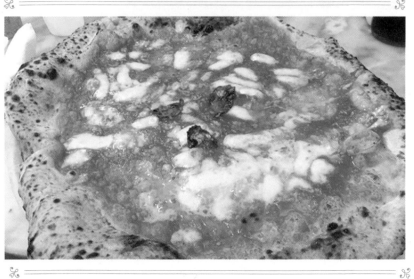

Naples, Italy

A Genuine Love Affair with Food

We should go to Naples on Valentine's Day," my husband excitedly exclaimed. Images of our time "passing through" Naples over the past five months flashed through my head. Naples is many things, including loud, seedy in places, dirty in still more places, and chaotic in a way I have never experienced. I didn't respond right away to his idea because I knew I would say something like, "NOT ON YOUR LIFE!" Instead I said, "Why?" His response was short and delicious: "Pizza."

I did expect to find the perfect pizza because Naples is the self-proclaimed birthplace of pizza. I did not expect to find a pulse in Naples that I truly enjoyed. It was in homage to Cupid, the Roman god of love. Huge, well-illuminated hearts lit up the cobblestoned streets in a way that would rival any large city at Christmas. There were posters in all the shop windows about the art of love, and there was a passion in the air that was, I believe, only possible in Naples. There were couples in heated discussions, hands flying, while zipping through traffic on their Vespas, matched only by those on park benches, kissing and gazing at one another as the silk rose bouquets drooped beside them on the bench. The only people more passionate than the couples we came across were the *pizzaiolos* (pizza makers).

The Associazione Verace Pizza Napoletana (True Neapolitan Pizza Association) was founded in 1984 to certify the *pizzerias* that are using the proper ancient artisan traditions of authentic pizza. The place to find the highest concentration of "certified" *pizzerias* is in the historic center of Naples on Via dei Tribunali. Some of the purist *pizzerias* we visited only serve two pizzas, the *Marinara* and the *Margherita*. Every ingredient is certified, as is each painstaking step to create the perfect pie! My husband is from the East Coast, and since the day I met him, has had a palpable fervor around artisan pizza. Growing up on the West Coast, Pizza Hut was my idea of good pizza. Hey, it was gourmet compared to the frozen-aisle variety! Today, of course, Seattle has some amazing *pizzerias*. Our favorite is called none other than Via Tribunali, on Capitol Hill.

I have to say, though, there was an earthy decadence to the pizza in Naples on Valentine's Day that had nothing to do with certifications or quality ingredients. It was all about love and how it infuses itself into food when we let it. "Buon San Valentino" is still coursing through me, and I owe it all to Naples (and to my husband).

Today I am deliberate in my love of food.

- What do you love to eat?
- Write a list now of anything that comes to mind quickly. Pick the most exciting thing on the list, and think about how you feel eating that food.
- Indulge yourself today for the love of food and the belief in the idea that your nourishment depends on it!

Today I am deliberate in my love of food because I know my health is directly related to how I feel about the food I eat.

notes

"There are moments in our lives when we summon the
courage to make choices that go against reason, against
common sense and the wise counsel of people we trust.
But we lean forward nonetheless because, despite all risks
and rational argument, we believe that the path we are
choosing is the right and best thing to do. We refuse
to be bystanders, even if we do not know exactly
where our actions will lead."

– Howard Schultz

Italy

Stop Seeking Approval for Your Dreams

Howard Schultz was a Starbucks employee in 1983 when he traveled to Italy and was enchanted, sip by sip, by the Italian coffee scene and its culture-defining rituals. When the founder of Starbucks decided to sell the company for 3.8 million, Schultz bought it. Without any idea how he would build on his vision, he said, "The passion was unbridled enthusiasm, desire, and the fact that I must do this." We all know what happened next.

Coffee in Italy is so much bigger than what is in the cup. The "coffee bar" culture here is about gathering. It is a place people come in the morning for a pastry and a *cappuccino*. Italians rarely drink coffee with any form of milk added after the morning cup. Italians then visit their local bar after *siesta* (sometime after 3 PM) and before *passeggiata* for espresso.

During *passeggiata* the *antipasti* is served, and the bar becomes a place for beer or grappa or brandy before dinner, which rarely begins before 8 PM. The bars are for everyone, young and old, rich and poor. Every Italian has his or her favorite bar, where they spend much of their day popping in and out in a way that connects everyone every day effortlessly.

One of the main differences between the coffee culture here and my past life at Starbucks is that you don't mess with coffee here. At Starbucks I always seemed to be caught behind the person who wanted the half-hazelnut, half-almond, half-caffeinated, sugar-free soy latte at 100 degrees. That drink would never get served in Italy. Once I learned how to "belly up" to the bar here, I quickly learned to order whether anyone was looking or not. I stood in awe as the artful cup, proud and perfectly caffeinated, steamed before me.

In Seattle, I was always on a mission for the perfect cup of coffee. I started as a child, following my mother to every corner of the Earth for espresso. She passed her passion on to me, and since being in Italy, I have changed the mission a bit. Now it is a game to see if I can find a bad cup of coffee. As I once followed my mother into the first espresso stands out west, my children dare me to try truck-stop coffee, Autostrada gas-station coffee, and the latest attempt—monastery vending-machine coffee. As I accept the dare, drop in my coins, and take the first sip, I am overwhelmed with a velvety goodness that melts my skeptical palate.

I have not found a bad cup of coffee in Italy. What I have found is a culture surrounding coffee that has made me feel at home in every coffee bar I have stepped foot in since arriving in Italy. I think in this regard, Howard Schultz achieved his dream. I think the difference is, in Italy every bar has a unique culture and family behind it. Yet although no two cups are the same, they are all made in the name of bringing people together, and that is something to celebrate.

Today I deliberately lean in the direction of a passion I harbor.

- Have you ever shared a dream with someone and taken their less-than-enthusiastic response to heart?

- Although you often look to others for approval of your dreams, it can be counterproductive because the dreams are your dreams. Instead, build faith in your own dreams by doing small things every day that add details to your vision.

- Today pick one dream that needs a reboot, and research something about it that breathes new life into your vision.

Today I deliberately lean in the direction of a passion I harbor because I know my dreams better than anyone.

notes

Matera, Italy

Making Room for What Matters Most

I will never forget foraging through the woods on our honeymoon, looking for our hotel in the Italian countryside, with hundreds of pounds of luggage knocking us this way and that. I swore, in that moment, I would never over-pack again. It only took me 12 years to keep that promise!

As we were preparing for this journey with three children, we came to a crossroads. We really wanted the freedom to go where we wanted, when we wanted, and luggage that needed to be hauled was not part of our vision. The question was: how do you go from 2500 square feet of stuff to five carry-on bags? We virtually pared our life down to a sliver of what we once owned in two months. The hardest part was that we knew we wanted to do many of the things we enjoyed while on the road, and some of those things required special equipment. What about ski gear, hiking boots, and biking? What do we do when we arrive in these beautiful landscapes and don't have what we need to enjoy the outdoors?

After many long conversations, we came to the conclusion that there is a cost to holding on to things we may need for every possible activity we want to partake in on any given day, whether we travel or stay put. We decided that we would borrow or buy anything we needed to enjoy whatever came about wherever we happened to be. This was a leap of faith, but it freed us from storing and shipping and packing for every contingency. Our five carry-on bags limited our accumulation of stuff with rigor.

We just left Southern Italy after three months, and those three months included Christmas and skiing. Typically, Christmas means adding a lot of stuff to the already stuffed storage. This year, the kids knew that everything they received was to be enjoyed while we were in that specific location. A magic thing happened. They took better care of their toys because there were fewer and they anticipated passing them on.

The night before we left the Basilicata region, we went to the town square, and the kids gave away the scooters they had lovingly washed and shined. They gave away sleds and dolls, play dough and puzzles. They had so much fun deciding who the lucky recipients would be, and all those conversations we had endured about the importance of giving back just clicked for them with no lecture. We have a completely different relationship to things. It is more of a fluid perspective versus a "keep it for a rainy day" view. We have borrowed ballet shoes, ski gear, bicycles, blenders, and soccer balls. We have borrowed binoculars, umbrellas, frying pans, and spices.

We have given as much as we have received, and we feel much lighter as a result. The things are temporary, and there will always be more or less depending on where we are in our life. For now, the freedom is priceless and has changed us from "holding on" to "moving through," and it is a lesson that applies to not only stuff, but to everything we once held on to for too long.

Today I am deliberate about letting go of things that are ready to move on.

- Fill one bag today with things you are ready to pass on.

- As you donate or dispose of its contents, visualize with excited anticipation what may fill the space you just had the courage to clear.

- Watch what shows up for you!

Today I am deliberate about letting go of things that are ready to move on because I know that clearing that space will make room for new treasures and adventures, and I am ready.

notes

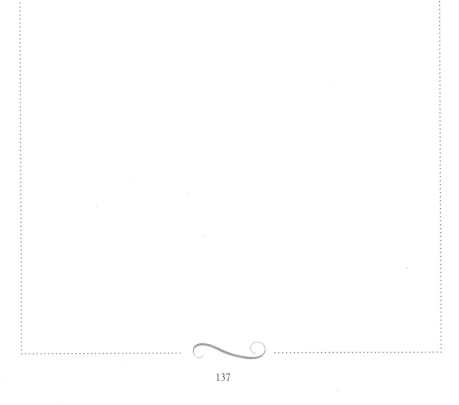

Pisa, Italy

The Meaning of Monuments: Pisa and Beyond

I have read so many travel pieces over the years that have suggested that one monument or another is not worth it due to the access, cost, or crowds. Monuments and major tourist attractions are worth it. They are worth it because they make you feel like you have arrived. The image from television, puzzles, screensavers, or childhood stories that you have dreamed about your entire life is right in front of you, and there is nothing better than that moment!

The sea of people flooding Pompeii, the switchback lines into the Coliseum, the torrential downpour and graffiti-ridden alleys leading to the Tower of Pisa, or the 15 toll booths on the way to Monaco are nothing compared to the moment you turn the corner and see it.

There is no way to describe the moment, no cost/benefit analysis that means anything. If it is a dream of yours to see the Eiffel Tower and the lines is six hours long, get a baguette and enjoy the journey. The only thing that matters is that you go if you dream of going.

In my experience, it is always worth it because it is so much bigger than the act. It is a lifetime fulfilled. It is an incalculable, monumental moment!

Today I deliberately articulate my dreams.

- Write down three places, monuments, or experiences you have always dreamed of. Your dream may be a Super Bowl game, an African safari, or a road trip.

- Close your eyes for even two minutes and picture how you feel during this experience. What do you see, hear, feel, and taste?

- Take that feeling into your day.

Today I deliberately articulate my dreams because I know that adding details to dreams is a critical part of them coming into my reality.

notes

Aix-en-Provence, France

Feeling the Explosion of Spring

I have never felt spring emerge the way I have in Aix-en-Provence. When we arrived, the plane trees were ghostly bare, and the shoppers at the outdoor markets were still bowing to the wind, heads down and tucked into beautiful French scarves.

In two short weeks, the shiver has been replaced by billowing trees and saffron-colored bouquets of the season's first blooms. Shoppers linger in the markets to listen to musicians while feasting on quiche Lorraine and sipping fruity *vin rosé*. Bulbs are pushing through with ferocious tenacity, and the wine makers are praying that no frost will follow the warmth of these early spring days.

Everyone is outside at any chance that arises for every possible moment. Cafés set up tables in every corner square, families tee-ter on the edge of fountains, and people-watchers perch on bar stools along the Cours Mirabeau.

What a glorious experience to witness spring beaming through the Provence countryside, all from the comfort of our temporary home in the Paris of the south, which locals simply call "X."

Today I deliberately witness the explosion of spring.

- Spend a few minutes today looking for spring!
- Can you hear rushing water where there was once silence? Is the rain less predictable and somehow sweeter? Does the sun have a new, youthful strength?
- Notice and see how you feel as the inspiration takes root within you.

Today I deliberately witness the explosion of spring because I know evidence of new growth is good for my soul.

notes

Le Luberon, France

Appreciating Beauty Makes You More Beautiful

France is one of the few places I have traveled where I feel like I was, in fact, born yesterday! Exploring the villages of Le Luberon and beyond was no exception. It is hard to describe the overwhelming sense that came over me that the French just have it figured out. Here is my evidence:

- In Bonnieux a visit to the Musée de la Boulangerie (bread museum), followed by a flawlessly executed warm *baguette* snack perched on a wall overlooking the valley floor, was the perfect way to start the day.

- After a slow walk through Goult for a late-morning *café au lait* at Café de la Poste, we felt like locals. Goult is not as popular among the tourists, and it was truly one of our favorite villages because we could see life happening around every sleepy corner.

- Gordes is officially one of The Most Beautiful Villages in France. It is always hard for something to deliver when it has that reputation, but Gordes does not disappoint. We loved watching the style in Gordes: families strolling near the imposing castle wall after church, mud-splattered mountain-bike riders taking their morning coffee after a vigorous ride through the hills, and couples that had been together for decades, arm in arm in their Sunday best. The style felt effortless and aspirational all at the same time.

- Roussillon is a Technicolor light show that Mother Nature puts on daily. Every hour that we spent exploring the ochre cliffs revealed a different shade and shadow of this majestic village. The style is grounded earning the village its place at the top of the must-see lists.

- Fontaine de Vaucluse and Les Baux are villages we spent time in outside Le Luberon, and they are just as fabulous in their entire splendor. The river that literally gushes up from the plateau and carves its way through Fontaine de Vaucluse is truly a sight. On a Thursday in March, we could not find parking in this popular gem. What we did find was a spot downstream where school children were lounging with their families for an afternoon picnic. We spread our blanket by the river and dined on fresh tapenade and red-pepper spread from the market in Les Baux.

- Les Baux literally took our breath away. The evidence of this village's numerous Renaissance periods were accentuated by the sensational natural landscape. The siege machinery and crossbow demonstrations at the medieval castle that crowns the village were a huge hit with our kids, and the view that has inspired artists the world over was an incredible backdrop. It was easy to understand how many leaders felt very powerful from their position atop Les Baux.

I love feeling like I have so much to learn from the French. The language, the fashion, the juxtaposition of the old and the new, and the subtle kindness of the people made for an experience full of grace and style that was truly enduring.

Today I am deliberate in my appreciation of beauty.

- Spend time today noticing beauty.

- It can be as simple as a sweater in a window display or as grand as a mountain peak gripping onto its snowcap.

- Behold each image for a second longer than you normally would, and see how your appreciation makes you more beautiful.

Today I am deliberate in my appreciation of beauty because I know that my ability to recognize it is a direct reflection of my belief in my inner radiance.

notes

"Look at that sea, girls—all silver and shadow and vision of things not seen. We couldn't enjoy its loveliness any more if we had millions of dollars and ropes of diamonds."

– L.M. Montgomery, *Anne of Green Gables*

Practicing the Art of a Day by the Sea

We have been to many seaside towns, villages, and cities during our stay in Provence, near the French Riviera. We had a picnic in Monte Carlo, ice cream in Saint-Tropez, a baguette in Antibes, and *apéritifs* in Cannes. We had a rock-skipping contest in Nice, a spin on the Ferris wheel in Marseille, and a swim next to gypsy caravans in Saints-Marie-de-la-Mer. We even wandered through the mythical marshlands in Camargue National Park, accompanied by the pink flamingos and white horses.

After all of these experiences, we determined during our day in Cassis that the French have mastered, and possibly invented, a day by the seashore. They come with their children, their lovers, and their friends. They come with their dogs, their music, and their *déjeuner gastronomique* (gourmet lunch). They come in style with navy-striped linen blouses, soft blankets, and a leisurely amount of time. The children ride on the Jules Verne vintage carousel as their parents sip wine perfumed by the sea.

There is a sense that the sun doesn't set until the French have completed their day *par la mer* (by the sea). As I sit worrying about dinner and what I will prepare, I realize just how much I have to learn about the seashore from this culture that has made it an art, as they have with so many things.

Today I am deliberate in my seaside reflections.

- Think of your favorite day by the sea. (If you have never been to the ocean, imagine your ideal day.)
- How was the weather? What did you hear, smell, do, and share?
- Take that breezy, relaxed, powerful feeling into your day.

Today I am deliberate in my seaside reflections because I know that I can recall those images any time I need a fresh perspective.

notes

Barcelona, Spain

Are You Ready for the Lessons That Surround You?

It is incredible to drive just a few hours in any direction and be in a different country, speaking a different language, with unique new flavors, and new vistas. Europe is incredible, in that we can just get in our car and drive into a completely new country with ease. We had big plans for Barcelona. Our kids did not! After two-plus incredibly active weeks in Provence, everyone was tired and feeling a bit uprooted when we arrived in the bustling capital of Catalonia. Barcelona has all of the Spanish tourist flare from *paella* to *flamenco*, but it has a distinctly complex, colorful, and proud Catalan past.

To understand it requires moving through Barcelona at a slower pace that allows the average visitor to catch the Catalan character. A local man told us there are two sides to the Catalan spirit, *el seny and la rauxa*. These two terms mean common sense and outburst, respectively. On one hand, hard work, diligence, and common sense are rewarded here, in contrast to the more *mañana* approach of other parts of Spain. On the other, you can see signs of *la rauxa* in Barcelona's unbeatable reputation as a cultural capital and a city of festivals and public art. The kids, in their rebellious exhaustion, revealed a side of Barcelona my original itinerary would not have allowed.

The 74-acre Parc de la Ciutadella forms a green oasis close to the always-crowded historic center of Barcelona. We sat on almost every bench, contemplated life along almost every promenade, and had the joy of listening to Catalan, the official tongue of Barcelona, while lounging underneath many palm-shaded stretches of grass. It is a Romance language spoken by nearly nine million people, and it is unlike anything we have heard before. We knew from the beginning that it was not Spanish or a Spanish dialect; it was a language of its own, with a history that has been making international headlines for quite some time.

While wandering through the maze of the historic center of Barcelona, tracing Picasso's early years, we were treated to a dance group practicing the steps of the *sardana*, the Catalan national folk dance. Like the language, we knew it was not *flamenco*. We knew it had a connection to the pulse of this city that was deep and rooted, as dancers locked arms with strength and purpose. We watched from outside the circle, unnoticed, and saw something we may have missed had I booked the "Flamenco Experience."

While walking in search of hot chocolate and churros, we passed many fairy-tale buildings by Antoni Gaudí. He was Catalan and facilitated the rise of Catalan architecture to worldwide fame and reputation. Gaudí was also an architect and designer with a special ability to synthesize his Catalan tradition with new technical solutions. The kids were so impressed by Sagrada Familia, Casa Batlló, and La Pedrera that they requested a visit to Park Güell where we spent lazy hours picnicking on the longest park bench in the world.

I can't imagine understanding Barcelona the way we do now, if the kids hadn't staged a protest! Their demonstration of independence and freedom from my itinerary was so very Catalonian in spirit!

Today I deliberately stop somewhere I typically rush through, to learn what it has to teach me.

- Spend 10 minutes today on a bench, in a cafe, or in your own home or garden, quietly observing your surroundings.

- What do you hear, smell, or appreciate today that you may sometimes miss during your daily routine?

- Today, take notice.

Today I deliberately stop somewhere I typically rush through, to learn what it has to teach me because the lessons are there when I am ready.

notes

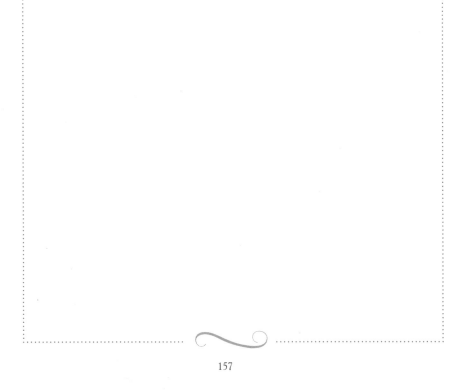

"He once told me that a story is a letter the author writes to himself, to tell himself things he would not be able to discover otherwise."

– Carlos Ruiz Zafon, *Shadow of the Wind*

Madrid, Spain

What Treasures Are Hiding Under Your Nose?

Even before arriving in Madrid, the flu descended on our family. I had visions of this historic capital that may never be realized. What we did experience was living in Madrid versus touring through it. Because our time was not shrouded in the glory of Palacio Real or crowned by the massive Goya canvases at the Prado Museum, the essence of this unique city revealed itself.

My Madrid was one of midnight mornings: Did you know that the palace changes from pearly white to effervescent silver as the sun rises? Did you know that if you sleepily wander into Chocolatería San Gines before 6 AM for hot chocolate and churros, you will be greeted by party-goers just bringing their evening to a close? Did you know that Puerto del Sol is truly radiant after a misty dawn? It is a beauty that does not reveal itself when the rest of the world is awake and crowds and trinket merchants blanket the square.

My Madrid was one of winsome *siestas:* Did you know that on Sunday afternoons, when all the *Madrilenes* (people of Madrid) have retreated for *siesta*, you may experience a virtually private opera or symphony performance by talented buskers practicing their craft? Did you know that after the fish markets close for lunch, you may be caught in the crossfire of local children having "snowball" fights with the ice left in piles outside the market stalls? Did you know that in La Latina (the oldest part of the city), the Church of San Francisco el Grande is the perfect spot to settle into a creaky pew and give thanks?

My Madrid was one of twilight expeditions: Did you know that *tapas* at San Miguel Market are an amazing representation of what the city has to offer in a breathtaking turn-of-the-century building of steel and glass construction? Did you know that as Plaza Mayor fills at night, you lose the symmetrical, rectangular sense of order you feel there during sleepy afternoons? Did you know that you can stand in the geographic center of Spain while in Madrid, and at night, as the city lights up, it truly feels like the world revolves around this illuminated metropolis?

Every time we left our apartment to find an open pharmacy or fresh fruit at the market, a new piece of this seductive city revealed itself to us. Without the glamorous, big attractions, we were gracefully enchanted by day-to-day life.

Today I am a deliberate explorer of the familiar.

- Have you ever gone out of town and returned seeing your home town in a new light, with enhanced appreciation?

- Today, look around you with a fresh perspective. What do you appreciate about where you are right now?

- Take that feeling into your day, and watch what wonder reveals itself.

Today I am a deliberate explorer of the familiar because I know that wonder is present if I just slow down.

notes

"For whatever we lose (like a you or a me)
it's always our self we find in the sea."

– E.E. Cummings

Algarve, Portugal

Can a Place Nourish You?

A week into our time along the southern coast of Portugal, we were just feeling a bit flat. After visiting the marina in Vilamoura, the seaside town of Olhos de Agua, and many inland castle towns, we just felt like we had seen it all before.

After fending off the dolphin and cave-tour clerk in Albufeira, we knew we were still searching. As we wound our way through whitewashed villages, passing saccharine fields of orange blossoms, we knew we were on our way to somewhere enchanting. As we approached the arduous steps to Falesia Beach, we finally knew why we traveled so far to reach the Algarve.

Falesia is only one of the many varied beaches that sweep the southern coast of Portugal, and there are many opinions as to which one is the best. My belief is that there is a beach for everyone because no two are alike. Falesia was our miracle mile—five miles actually! The tawny cliffs were ablaze with spring wildflowers. Blooms in every hue tumbled to the crashing Atlantic, where their fall was broken by liquid-gold sand as far as the eye could see. The sand was strong enough to withstand a good breeze, but creamy to the touch and perfect for castles.

We could not bring ourselves to leave. We toyed with the surf, hiked along the cliffs, followed endless trails slicing through canyons, and settled on the now-empty beach chairs to watch the sun set and the moon rise simultaneously. With our hands sticky from our bag of freshly picked oranges that had nourished us all day long, we began our hike back to our car. We were quiet, as a feeling of contentment settled over us; a feeling that only comes from knowing the search is over ... until tomorrow.

Today I deliberately honor a place I feel nourished in mind, body, and spirit.

- Visualize the first place that comes to your mind when you think of nourishing your mind, body, and spirit.

- Picture yourself there, and listen for a minute to your memory. You can access this place any time, day or night, because you discovered it within you, before you found it in the world.

- It is yours!

Today I deliberately honor a place I feel nourished in mind, body, and spirit, because I know how special such places are and yet how accessible.

notes

Libson, Portugal

Watch and Learn

Portugal feels very foreign. We have been in many foreign countries, but this is the first time we have no frame of reference or foundation of familiarity. The language, the food, the customs, and the landscape are all new. Because of this heightened sense of awareness, we rely heavily on the power of observation.

At the grocery store in Cascais, we watched the women as they did their shopping. Are they touching the produce? Are they using gloves? Is there a scale for customers or does the clerk weigh the goods? At the flea market in Sintra, we watched families shop. Are they bartering, or is that insulting? Are they touching or just looking? How is business started and ended? Is anyone speaking English? What gestures do they use for yes and no?

As we entered a church in the heart of Lisbon for Easter mass, so many things were familiar: children wearing their Easter best, the smell of incense, and standing room only as families crammed into this sacred space. The rhythm of the mass was comforting. The Lord's Prayer in Portuguese had the same cadence and meditative power. "Peace be with you" connected us to other parishioners, even though we were speaking a different language. We understood nothing and everything. The power of observation helped us spend a magical Easter in a Catholic country with ease.

We have been wielding this new power for many months through many countries, but we have only just realized how invaluable it has become. We hope we never forget how much can be gained by entering a new store, home, business, relationship, city, country, or culture with thoughtful observation, versus posturing or defining words. Words have their own magnificent power, but sometimes, we have noticed, they can be diminishing if they are spoken with haste.

Enter, observe, question, understand, and act with grace. That is our new order of things.

Today I am a deliberate observer.

- As you enter into interactions today, practice your power of observation.

- Notice where others are coming from and going to, and quietly wish them well.

- Listen to understand, and watch how magically you feel more understood by the world.

Today I am a deliberate observer because I want to come from a place of love and understanding in all interactions.

notes

"I would not like to live in a world without cathedrals.
I need their beauty and grandeur. I need them against the
vulgarity of the world. I want to look up at the illuminated
church windows and let myself be blinded by the unearthly colors ...
I want to let myself be wrapped in the austere coolness of
the churches. I need their imperious silence ... I want to hear the
rustling of the organ, this deluge of ethereal tones. I love praying
people. I need the sight of them. A world without these things
would be a world I would not like to live in."

– Pascal Mercier, *Night Train to Lisbon*

Santiago de Compostela, Spain

A Different Kind of Pilgrimage: Santiago de Compostela

As we approached the cathedral of Santiago de Compostela, I started to cry. It is a magical place where pilgrims from all over the world celebrate their journey. Children were singing, elderly were praying on their knees, couples were hugging, Girl Scout troops were beaming for pictures, and a few solitary pilgrims were on the outskirts, reflecting on their reasons for being in this place in this moment. There was a moment when I felt like we didn't belong. We haven't walked the El Camino for days or weeks or months. We parked in the parking garage a mile away.

As I stood there, with my husband and children, and listened to the pilgrims' song, I remembered that just that morning we were in a different country; that just in the last week we were speaking a different language; that in the last month we have crossed continental coasts; that in the last eight months we have spent time in seven countries. It was then that I knew why the pilgrims' song rang true.

We are on a different kind of journey, and we should stop, celebrate, reflect, listen, and most of all, give thanks. Every pilgrim has a different reason for setting out. One thing about this moment of "crossing the finish line" that will always stay with me is that there is a profound knowledge that once you start seeking, there is no finish line.

Today I deliberately celebrate my journey.

- Spend a moment, now if you can, reflecting on where you have been.

- Give thanks for the journey and the lessons along the way (good and bad) that are a part of who you are today.

- Take the strength of that adventure into your day.

Today I deliberately celebrate my journey because I know giving thanks for how far I have come is just as important as where I am headed.

notes

*"France may one day exist no more,
but the Dordogne will live on just as dreams
live on and nourish the souls of men."*

– Henry Miller

Dordogne, France

Are You a Little Bit Country?

Every day in my travel research, I come across the terms hidden gem, off the beaten path, unspoiled, authentic, and undiscovered. The Dordogne region of France is the only place I have been thus far where it is actually true.

Castles sit like crown jewels along the river banks. We often found ourselves beating our own path through the oak forests toward the river bank. The countryside looks much the same as it has for hundreds of years, with emerald-green farms held down by Perigord chateaus.

As far as authenticity, the gas station shop sells local *pâté* and *foie gras*, and on more than one occasion, we were greeted by villagers going about their daily routines. Although the Perigord Noir region we explored has been well-known for decades by the English, Dutch, and Belgians as a summer-home locale, there is still a preserved peace that settles over the region, even its most popular corners.

Each day was a feast for the senses. The earthy aroma of the dewy mornings gracefully gave way to the gentle spring breeze kissing the endless fields. As we rowed past castles dreams are made of, the whoosh of the crinoline from days gone by was almost audible. We found hermetic places to beach our boats, where the aroma of goose-liver pâté, truffles, and wild walnuts perfumed the banks where we picnicked.

From Beynac to Limeuil we were surrounded by ochre fields set against new spring leaves and butterscotch-colored stone homes that looked like they had graced the hillside forever. The deafening birdsong at sunset was the perfect accompaniment for our efforts to take in every last moment of light offered.

I could not help but think that the Dordogne felt like one of those places that people hide from others once they discover it. I could not think of another reason for it not being flooded with people from every corner of the world. It is unique, timeless, affordable, and precious. It was everything we wanted it to be and so many things we could not have imagined.

Today I am deliberate in my appreciation of the countryside.

- What images come to mind when you think of pastoral country life?
- What colors, sounds, and tastes assault your memory?
- Take the best of those memories, and know that you can retreat there whenever you need a deep breath.

Today I am deliberate in my appreciation of the countryside because I know its openness is within me when I need a fresh perspective.

notes

"What does it depend on when we have experienced a month
as a fulfilled time, our time, instead of a time that has
passed us by ... that ran through our fingers, so that it seems
to us like a lost, past time, and we're not sad because it is past,
but because we couldn't do anything with it? So, the question
was not how long is a month, but rather: What can you do
for yourself with the time of a month? When is it that I have the
impression that this month was all mine? The fullness of time
that yawns when the barrage of appointments falls silent?
Aren't those wonderful things? A heavenly situation?
So why the fear of it?"

– Pascal Mercier, *Night Train to Lisbon*

Giverny, France

The Art of Cherishing One's Self

Mother's Day always used to feel a little awkward. It was a day I looked forward to with expectations that were never fulfilled because wanting to be appreciated never sets anyone up for success. A wise French woman in Paris explained to me that it is very important for women in this culture to care for themselves a bit every day. That way, they have more energy and beauty to bring to all those they come into contact with throughout the day. I walked away from the conversation believing what she said to be true but not comprehending how to put her wisdom into practice.

Before this journey, I was well versed in sacrificing my time, my energy, and my physical health for others, and I felt tired. I looked up as I walked the streets of Paris. I could see evidence of cherishing oneself everywhere. It was not just the extrinsic, effortless style but a sense of self that I had rarely felt in the past. There was a rhythmic pace and relaxed joy that was palatable in many women I observed. It wasn't something one could fake, at least not in my experience.

I realize now after over 250 days on the road, it is more important to take care of oneself a bit every day than to expect others to fill the dry well one day a year. Since we have been traveling, I take time each day to exercise, to write, and to play. I take time to be present and to give back, and I take time to give thanks.

Every day leading up to Mother's Day this year, I spent time in appreciation of myself, my family, and my surroundings. I came into it with a "fullness of time," as Mercier states, and no anxiety that the day needed to be special because it was the only day of the year for ME (and my mother)! The result was that the well overflowed. As I sat in Monet's garden at Giverny, listening to spring crackle all around me, I was penetrated by this knowledge that it was the little things each day that had led me to this moment. It was not the big decisions to sell everything, to travel as a family, and to apply for dual citizenship. It was the daily practices of gratitude, joy, and self-care that had made this month, this year, this journey, and especially this day feel like it was "all mine."

The irony is that I was always expecting the appreciation to come from others, and it turned out it was a gift only I could give myself.

Today I am deliberate in my appreciation of myself.

- Do one thing for yourself today that contributes to you feeling cherished. Maybe it is a lingering bath, a lunch date, a candlelight dinner, or a special purchase.
- Pick something that feels good from every angle and soak it up!

Today I am deliberate in my appreciation of myself because I know how to take care of me better than anyone.

notes

*"It wasn't exactly despair they were feeling;
it was more like a refusal to understand, the stupor you feel
when you're dreaming, when the veil of sleep is about to lift,
when you can feel the dawn light, when your whole body
reaches out towards it, when you think,
'It was just a nightmare, I'm going to wake up now.'"*

– Irene Nemirovsky, *Suite Française*

Normandy, France

Questions Are More Important Than Answers

As we stumbled into the sunlight in Arromanches, after viewing a 360-degree movie with never-before-seen footage of D-Day and the 100 days following, Gold and Juno beach were right before our eyes. There was an audible silence, and then the kids made the connection that the tanks, the soldiers, the air raids, and all that chaos occurred right on this sparkling, sun-drenched beach 70 years ago. Our son whispered, "It doesn't seem possible that all that happened right here. It doesn't seem like anything that awful could happen in such a beautiful place." As we drove through the villages toward Omaha and Utah beach, we passed bombed-out walls, and the kids pointed at schoolhouses that were partially re-built. It was hard to comprehend so much destruction in such a peaceful area, full of birdsong and turning plows.

They fired questions:

- Do you think it was good to have all that fighting so someone bad like Hitler didn't stay in power?
- Do you think Hitler would have ever been in power without WWI?
- Do you think war has to happen?
- What wars are happening now?
- How do they start?
- How do you know when they are over?
- Who wins?
- How do you know who wins?

We spent a lot of time just listening to the questions. They are age-old questions, and there are so many answers.

As we crested the hill in the American Cemetery in Colleville-Sur-Mer, our oldest son looked at the sea of white marble crosses and said, "I am glad Hitler didn't win, but it looks like everyone lost something."

We hiked up to the church on the cliffs above the alabaster arches in Etretat and had a picnic. As we looked out to sea, our current vistas veiled with historic overlays, we felt full of gratitude for this moment of peace, for this overwhelming restored beauty, and for experiences that lead to new questions.

Today I deliberately ask new questions.

- Write down three questions you have today for which you do not have the answer.
- Put thought into the questions and simply accept that because they have been asked, you will live your way into the answer.

Today I deliberately ask new questions because I know that my willingness to learn is directly related to the quality and sincerity of my questions.

notes

"Not everything can be
important, and not always,'
I said. 'That would be awful.'"

– Pascal Mercier

Paris, France

Paris: Go Deep or Go Wide

When we sat down to make our list of "Things to Do" in Paris, the conversation ended with everyone feeling overwhelmed, anxious, and tired, and we weren't even there yet! It led to a much more meaningful conversation about why we feel like we are missing something if we do not see everything. Where does that belief come from? Is that mindset serving us on this journey? Has it ever served us to cram? How do we change it?

When we really took the time to reflect on what was most meaningful in our lives, we came to the conclusion that it was about the experience more than checking things off the list. We agreed that when we try to cover too much ground, we end up not really "touching" anything in a meaningful and memorable way. We narrowed the list from 53 things to do in Paris to three.

I had moments of panic when we had free time. I wanted to fill it with a quick trip to Rodin or a riverboat cruise. I am so glad we didn't. The free time gave us something we have rarely experienced. It gave us time to process the experience while we were still in it. It was remarkable to have time to savor the anticipation of our chosen sights. We talked about climbing the stairs up the Eiffel Tower for days. We wondered how it would feel to have the wind whip through the iron. We speculated about the difficulty and about how it would feel to ascend such a structure.

It was equally novel to give ourselves the luxury to reminisce and tell stories about an experience that was still happening. As we sat at the top of the Notre Dame cathedral, after climbing the tower one worn marble step at a time, we talked about the personalities of the gargoyles. We wondered how anyone could have ever rung so many bells by hand. We discussed the view from the top of the cathedral and how different it was from the Eiffel Tower vista.

As for museums, we picked the Louvre. Yes, we narrowed it down, but the Louvre itself is a bit daunting. How can we simplify it even more? We invested in a beautifully executed scavenger hunt and walk through history designed for kids ages 6–12. Our guide was completely focused on engaging our children and teaching them about history by placing them in it as often as possible. We talked, we compared, and we laughed, and we had nowhere else to be but exactly where we were.

Our time in Paris had me thinking about how I would apply depth versus breadth to my life, as I knew it before this journey. I often crammed in vacation, crammed in summer camps, crammed in healthy meals and snacks, before running to the next thing. I think that at the center of my cramming was the fear of missing something. What I now know is that I was missing it because I was cramming.

I will never forget Paris. What a beautiful place to learn such an important lesson. If we had not crossed out 50 things on our list, we would have missed it.

livit

Today I deliberately tell the story of my day.

- Gather morsels of a good story today. Prepare to share the story of your day with someone (or write it down before bed).

- The more you build your own story, the more you will own the happy endings and new beginnings.

Today I deliberately tell the story of my day because giving my experience a framework contributes to my understanding and my legacy.

notes

summer

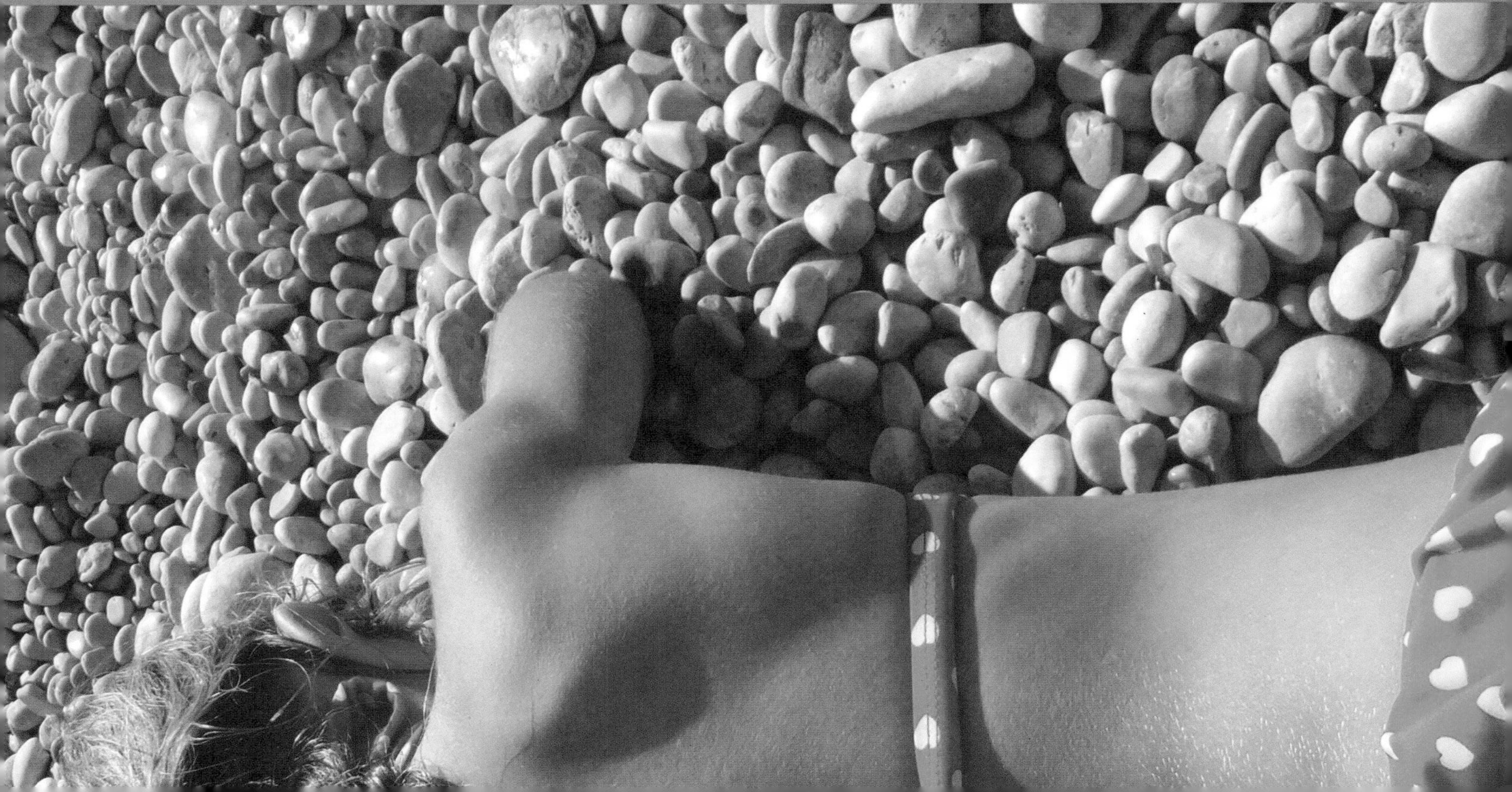

"A mother is not a person to lean on,
but a person to make leaning unnecessary."

– Dorothy Canfield Fisher

Lac de Chalain, France

What Motherhood and Rites of Passage Have in Common

As we launched our canoes on Lac de Chalain in the late afternoon, a thick, milky veil clouded my vision. How did we end up here, in this perfect moment, on this perfect day? We never planned to come to the Jura Mountains in France. When the weather turned in Normandy, we were off, and we picked a spot that we could get to in a day. We didn't know anything about the region, but we knew enough about France to know that it would be spectacular.

The Lac de Chalain is a natural glacier-fed lake and has been visited for centuries. The first traces of man living on its shores date from 3,600 years BC. There are parts of the lake where on a clear day, you can see remains of ancient civilizations that are now archeological gems. Because of this, the lake and its perimeter is a protected zone (the use of motorized boats is prohibited), which contributes to the tranquility of the area. It is the largest of the Jura lakes, and it is radiant.

We decided it was the perfect time for the boys to have their own vessel. Every other time we have been in a boat, one of us has been with them. This was the perfect setting for that important rite of passage, like the first bike, or the first day of school. When they said, a bit hesitantly, "Can we go in our own boat?" We replied, "Of course." There were moments of arguing, synchronizing paddling without going in circles, and trying to work together to gain traction, but it was only minutes before the proud smiles dominated. They had systems. They were laughing and talking about their adventures in the past year, while pointing out fish, loons and other birds.

Like only children can, they started dreaming about living their whole life on the water because they loved the moment they were in with such passion. What if we had a house right up there and we rowed every day? What if we knew every corner of this lake and we gave tours? What if we found another civilization at the bottom of the lake that no one has discovered yet?

They cut across the water as the sun was dipping, and they had a new sense of self. As they ventured farther away, it became easier for them and yet harder for me.

Today I deliberately honor milestones that contributed to my growth.

- Recall one memory that changed the course of your experience because of your courage to venture into the unknown.

- What was present in your life at that time that made the risk worthwhile?

- What opportunities might present themselves today, and what will you do?

Today I deliberately honor milestones that contributed to my growth because I know remembering those experiences gives me courage to continue to take risks.

Italian Alps

When Was the Last Time You Felt Like a Kid in a Candy Store?

What is better than being a kid in a candy store? How about being a kid living above an authentic pizzeria at the base of the Matterhorn in the Italian Alps! Lino's Pizzeria in Cervinia was pure magic.

My husband lived in Cervinia twenty years ago and emailed Lino for lodging suggestions. When Lino offered his place, we replied, graciously declining, as we are a family of not two or three, but five! "The more the merrier," was his sentiment, and he was sincere. Not only did he welcome the kids but he celebrated them. Because it was off-season, they got to not just "play restaurant" but be servers, sous chefs, and bartenders. The idea of living above a restaurant was so romantic for them, and the fact that Lino worked around the clock did not register in their beaming smiles, as they woke him every morning at dawn. Lino would help the kids make *cappuccini* for us, served bedside. He would assist them gently as they tossed their pizza dough, and he would let them write down their orders and take them to the kitchen. They washed dishes, set tables, swept floors, and cleared with glee. It is worth noting these are all chores they do with slightly less enthusiasm when we are not living above a restaurant.

The Matterhorn was nearly close enough to touch. The crack of the glacier was almost audible. We weathered rain, snow, and the brightest sun on earth. Lino's business is weather-dependent, so the kids caught the hang of anticipating more customers when the sun was shining. As they collapsed each night, the din of the customers laughing and glasses clinking lulled them to sleep. Lino's generous spirit and unconditional hospitality was unforgettable. We picked bursting cherries in his parents' garden. We walked on paths with timeless alpine meadows and vistas. We listened to the Franco-Provençal dialect of Patois, and we heard stories only mountain men can share about great ascents, the ebb and flow of mountain villages, and the families that live and die at the base of such majesty.

It is safe to say we pick prosciutto and arugula pizza over the candy store any day!

Today I deliberately pretend.

- What did you dream of as a child? Did you want to be a fireman or own a pastry shop? Did you want to live in a castle or a treehouse?

- Remember for a moment what it felt like to believe it was possible. What is the new dream? No one is watching, so go BIG in honor of your dreams!

Today I deliberately pretend in ways that inspire my imagination and ignite my dreams, old and new.

notes

"Only those who risk going too far can possibly find out how far they can go."

– T. S. Eliot

Molise, Italy

New Appreciation for Something Familiar

Have you ever returned from a vacation and noticed things about home with new appreciation, or even noticed things for the first time? This journey for us has been a series of one-way tickets, and last week was our first experience "returning" in over eight months.

We ventured back to the Molise region of Italy to complete our citizenship paperwork. When we arrived in Molise back in October, we were just beginning our wandering ways, and we were trying to figure out language, groceries, and traffic laws.

This time, with a bit more confidence, we entered the region with our eyes wide open, and the experience was completely different. We saw verdant fields carpeted with poppies. Bales of hay perched on valley floors as if they had just rolled down on a hot summer day. Local cuisine, such as *scamorza* cheese and *porchetta* sandwiches tasted home-cooked and comforting. How could something be so familiar and so new with every breath?

I realized that it is impossible to see the same place the same way twice because each time we venture, we grow, and growth changes everything. Whether we travel from one destination to the next, or take a vacation and fly home, there is no returning. There is only ever-forward movement. Perhaps that innate knowledge is what makes it hard to go sometimes.

I think at some level we know that nothing will be the same upon our return, including ourselves. There are always a million things that prevent us from "getting away" if we let them, but when we do leave, we realize growth is invigorating and scary and necessary. The best part is, it makes returning so much sweeter.

Today I am deliberate in acknowledging that I am in charge of how I show up.

- Think of how you show up somewhere familiar today. Do you see others with wonder or a predictable hello? Do you go through the motions, or do you look up and really see things in the new light that is being offered?

- Try to leave behind your preconceived notions about the way things or people should be.

- Watch how many people and places you thought were done surprising you, were in fact only just beginning.

Today I am deliberate in acknowledging that I am in charge of how I show up, and each time I return, I am changed by having left.

notes

Rome, Italy

Gladiator School: What History Knows That You May Have Forgotten

We covered the history of the church in Rome. We covered architectural marvels such as the Pantheon and the Coliseum. We studied daily life in the Forum and *piazzas* but we avoided glorifying the gladiator as long as possible. On our second trip to Rome, nine months after the first, the gladiator took center stage. We knew it was time to jump into this part of history with our heads up, or look the other direction.

What more do nine and ten-year-old boys need to engage in history than re-enacting condemned men's battles to the death with exotic animals and fellow criminals? It was important for the kids to understand the gladiator's role in Ancient Rome starting in the 3rd century, and why there is an allure still surrounding these warriors today. I also knew I was not the one to teach them, so we signed up for Gladiator School as a family.

We learned about the first forms of what we know today as psychological warfare and chemical warfare and how closely related the gladiator tradition was to the Roman soldiers. We were taught how to attack, how to defend, and how to die with honor while touching, wearing, and feeling the weight of artifacts from this time in history.

I am grateful to the gladiators for being a portal to jump through with my children that engaged them enough to want to devour the complex and layered history of Ancient Rome. I don't think anything less glamorous or rogue could have attracted them with the same tenacity.

What I learned is not to look away. Every piece of history, no matter how sordid, is a gateway to a deeper understanding of the path that leads to now.

Today I deliberately appreciate my history.

- What are the main events from your past that define you? Are these things you feel inspired thinking about, or do they cause stress?

- Try today, while acknowledging all of your history as important, to connect with memories that propel and inspire you into your day.

Today I deliberately appreciate my history as a portal into my current knowledge of myself and my passions.

notes

"Reject the tyranny of being picked: pick yourself."

– Seth Godin

Rome, Italy

Rather Than Waiting to Be Picked, Pick Yourself

I was desperately in search of Wi-Fi last week to see if my latest pitch had been accepted by a new publisher. With three kids in tow in a foreign country, I felt like a crazy person. Why am I so attached to this? They are offering a pittance, and that is if I am the lucky one. I felt like I was in third grade, praying not to be picked last for the kickball team.

It was then that I realized that I have been culturally trained to wait to get picked. I waited to hear back from colleges and graduate schools. I sent countless résumés into the abyss and waited. I waited at job fairs and plowed through interview waiting areas. Many times I was picked, many times I was not, but neither felt quite right.

Almost every day since we left on this journey, we have "picked" ourselves. We go where we want, when we want to, and we feel empowered every day. Because of this freedom, the idea of going back to "Pick me!" felt jarring, damp, and heavy. I came away from this contrast grateful for the knowledge that I do not need permission to pick myself; I have always had the resources I need to do just that. I do not have to wait. I can publish anything, anytime.

The magic is that as soon as I decided to pick myself over waiting to be picked, the offers came flooding in. The best part is that it is much more fun than the waiting game and much more profitable. I love the concept of picking ourselves because we have all waited to be picked for something: jobs, relationships, teams, promotions, schools. I think sometimes it is easier to wait because then when we aren't picked, we can blame some external factor.

There is accountability, excitement, and fear in picking oneself, and because of that there is a liberating boundlessness that propels us forward. There is no turning back. The freedom is wonderfully frightening and becomes the only palatable choice. It is a decision, every day, to pick oneself.

Today I deliberately pick myself.

- Think of one area of your life where you are waiting to be picked. Is it a promotion, a relationship, a board position, a career change, a friendship?

- Pick yourself. What does it mean to pick yourself? It means you are deciding to take back the power, dream up the life, job, relationship, or friendship you most desire without any attachment to the outcome.

- Watch how picking yourself swings open doors you didn't even know existed.

Today I deliberately pick myself because I know that the greatest risks reap the greatest rewards, and I have the courage to own my path.

notes

Rome, Italy

How to Steal the Show By Keeping an Open Mind

It was Talent Show Night. If you have ever been a six-year-old girl or had a six-year-old girl, you know how important Talent Show Night is in their world. We are staying at a family bungalow resort near Rome, and it is like summer camp for the kids. There are kids from all over the world to play with every day and wonderful camp counselors that organize games and shows for the kids to take part in.

After a balmy 88-degree day, the skies opened up, and the tears started to fall. "There is no talent show if it rains," the girls cried. My daughter and her friends from Germany, Italy, and Holland had coordinated a few dances together over the past week. They all worked tirelessly to overcome massive language barriers and communication breakdowns, and they couldn't believe a storm was ruining everything.

A quick-thinking camp counselor decided to move the show from the outdoor stage into the bar. The scene that followed will be part of our Italian experience forever. It was 9 PM before the talent show was all set up and ready. By this point the World Cup game was on, and the bar was packed at this little family resort.

As my daughter and her friends performed their Macarena and Gangnam Style routines, happy-hour soccer fans cheered them on, clapping with all their might. The girls twirled and sang, surrounded by strangers from all over the world who watched them like great aunts and uncles would have in a kitchen growing up. The girls beamed as the crowd yelled, "Brava, Bien fait! Gut Gemacht!" When they were done, the lady at the bar gave them gelato, and they sat and watched the game for a bit to cool down among their new fans.

I could not help but think how amazing it is that our children feel like they are part of a world community now. They always have been, as we all are, but they feel it now. They don't have any cultural expectations for things to go a certain way, because many of their friends are from different cultures. It did not even phase my daughter that spinning to "Hey, sexy lady" from Gangnam Style, in a bar, after 10 PM, would not have been part of her life in the United States.

They come into things wide open because they have no preconceived notions for how things are done in Italy, Spain, France, Germany, or Holland.

It struck me, as I was watching this talent show that the first step in becoming a global citizen is stripping away the preconceptions of how things should be in order to see things for what they are.

Today I am deliberately open to new experiences.

- Leave the word "should" out of your vocabulary today.

- When the "shoulds" start creeping in, think about what you want to do rather than what you should do, and try following that inspiration while allowing others the same courtesy.

- Try to take a break from how things should be in order to see the magic in what is before you.

Today I am deliberately open to new experiences because I want to be able to discover surprises even in things that may appear predictable.

notes

Rome, Italy

What Does it Mean to Declare Independence?

Many questions arise about roots and if our children's sense of belonging is compromised by a more nomadic lifestyle.

We believe each place we spend time, we leave a part of ourselves. When we establish real relationships with people, roots take hold naturally and in the most unforeseen places. Our roots are far-reaching, casting a global canopy that will give our kids independence and infinite hearths to return to when a homecoming seems imminent or inspired.

Our roots are harder to see. They no longer require a picket fence or an address, as we once believed. It is not that we didn't feel at home with those things, but that was not what made it home. What made it home was the time we spent together behind that fence, at that address.

Time we once spent mending fences or shopping for a better address, we now spend together, exploring the world. There may be many more picket fences in our future, but we no longer need them to feel at home.

The beauty of intrinsic roots is that once they take hold, no one can rattle their presence or impede the fence line, because it has little to do with real estate and everything to with feeling grounded anywhere.

It is the ultimate sense of freedom to be home the moment we arrive. That I do declare!

Today I am deliberately at home.

- What feelings do you associate with being "home?" Write them down.

- Those feelings are possible from anywhere, anytime, and require no physical geographic location.

- When you need to center yourself today, "go home" in your mind and heart, and watch how your day transforms.

Today I am deliberately at home because I know that what grounds me about home comes from within and is accessible to me from anywhere.

notes

"Let us make a special effort to stop communicating with each other, so we can have some conversation."

– Mark Twain

Rome, Italy

What Europeans Know About the Art of Conversation

For the first time ever, we spent our wedding anniversary dinner with our children. We didn't even think to celebrate without them. Why? Because they have learned a great deal about the art of conversation and dining from Europeans. It is an art our parents instilled in us at a young age but that we lost track of as our calendars overflowed.

Prior to our anniversary dinner, we were talking to a resort director about the concept of babysitting. He has two grown children, and he and his wife still take care of their respective parents. He kept asking questions about babysitting, and finally he said, bewildered, "So you pay NOT to be with your children?" We thought a great deal about his comment. It is fascinating that different cultures have such different ideas about family, especially about children and aging parents.

I remember waiting on the front steps for babysitters to arrive and giving them instructions as I ran past them, handing off babies and toddlers. What has changed? For one, I didn't want to sit in a McDonald's or Chuck E. Cheese to dine with my husband while the kids played. It is easy to go out with the entire family in many parts of Europe, especially Italy. It is expected. Generations go to lunch, dinner, or parties. There are play structures, fields, toys, puppet shows, magic shows, anything shows, that allow families to spend time eating four or five courses over two to three hours almost every day!

The other major difference is that meal time is about conversation. Our children will now sit for over an hour and talk at the dinner table. We noticed this change after about six months in Italy. They learned the art of conversation from many European friends, and we know our children better because of the meals we share. In France they learned not to snack. When they arrived to the table, they were hungry and would sit, eat, and talk. In Spain they learned how to enjoy various performances while mostly snacking, tapas-style. In Italy they have mastered the art of slowing down at meal time and savoring each course.

There are plenty of adults who will pinch their cheeks and try to scoop them up as they play with other kids between courses. They all return joyfully when the next course is ready. Adults have time together while kids are having fun, and the essence of the "family restaurant" finally makes sense to me. It is served family-style, in a family-friendly place, to the entire family!

After our incredible anniversary dinner, we had gelato at a store that also sold handmade leather shoes. That's *Amore!*

Today I am deliberate about my appreciation of gathering at the table.

- Take time today to dine with someone you care about. It may be your family or a dear friend or neighbor.

- The key is to be able to sit and experience the intimacy of being around the table. It does not matter what you eat, but it matters that you stay long enough for the experience to settle in around you.

- It is an art, and it will make you feel more nourished if you let it in.

Today I am deliberate about my appreciation of gathering at the table because I know that when I am present at the table, the food is more nourishing in every way.

notes

Rome, Italy

When Is it Time to Remember?

This past month we have focused on redesigning, reinventing, revising, and restoring, but what we will take with us from this time is the overwhelming feeling that it was time to remember.

As my husband built our new website, we had many discussions about what to take forward and what to leave behind. During these conversations, we sifted through photos, past stories, and comments from our readers. By looking back, we saw the little changes that we may not have noticed every day. We saw subtle glimpses into our children's growth, news from back home about weddings and births, and photos of surreal landscapes we have traversed.

The process of remembering is a grounding and dreamlike dance. It is also a creative process to remember, as we sort and experience the emotions certain memories evoke. We are, in a sense, selecting what to keep alive within us.

We talked about how, at times in the past, we have felt burdened by memories or obligated to remember certain things out of some sort of fear of repeating the same mistakes twice. The Latin origin of remember is *memorari,* and it means to be mindful. What we have learned in this process is that it was our choice to bring any and all memories forward, for better or for worse.

We have noticed that often before huge leaps forward, we pause to glance at all that has come before. It is not permission we are seeking, but strength and momentum to take a new step into an uncertain place. To be mindful is the greatest of gifts, as the images and voices of the past gently guide and accompany us into the unknown and give us the courage to remember our way into our next big adventure.

Today I am deliberately mindful.

- Spend just a few minutes this weekend remembering. Pull out a photo album, virtual or otherwise. Call a relative or pull a forgotten box down from a dusty shelf.

- As you sift, pay attention to what emotions you have toward the memories you are recalling. If you are inspired, purge things that you no longer wish to bring forward.

- At the same time, relish in the smell of baby clothes that have been packed away, or look closely at a yellow-tinted, old-fashioned letter! Listen to stories with a different awareness.

- Take a few minutes to notice and honor the reasons for these keepsakes.

Today I am deliberately mindful of my past and what I intentionally call forward into my present and future.

notes

Rome, Italy

Do You Have All the Answers?

What is the answer? I know the answer! You got four out of five answers correct! Answer me! Did you answer the question?

Many chapters in my life have been about learning, knowing, and bestowing answers. I often feel like I am searching for certain answers while imparting others to employees, students, or my children.

Travel has taught me that I have been looking for and sharing answers, when solutions are so much more universal. Every culture produces different solutions to similar problems. There are no "straight answers" and very little agreement or disagreement, just a diversity of solutions.

- Answers communicate certainty; solutions communicate a desire for understanding.

- Answers tell; solutions collaborate.

- Answers are finite; solutions are evolutionary.

- Answers are something we search for outside of ourselves; solutions require a part of us and are participatory.

- Answers are black and white, right and wrong; solutions are a situational shade of luminous grey.

- Answers want to be looked for; solutions beg for discovery.

Finding a solution means that I have accurately identified a problem that needs to be solved, and by that point I am 99% of the way! Asking for answers, or demanding them as I sometimes do, means I don't yet know what I am looking to solve because I am still outside of myself.

Solution-seekers are the wave of the future because they have clarity about the problem, courage to participate, and the unyielding knowledge that there are many truths.

Today I am deliberate in my desire to be a part of the solution.

- Articulate a problem that exists for you.
An example may be, "Why does my boss take credit for my work?"

- Now rewrite the problem by putting yourself in it. "Why is it important for me to be recognized by others for the work I do?"

- Try answering both questions briefly. Where answering the first question diminishes your power, answering the second question propels you into ownership of the solution.

Today I am deliberate in my desire to be a part of the solution because I know that accountability is empowering.

notes

Rome, Italy

What Are Your Favorite Subjects?

The teacher in me always asks kids, "What are your favorite subjects in school?" All over the world, to date, the majority of kids say, "Lunch and recess."

Here is what we have learned from a year of spending a great deal of time at lunch and recess:

- Sharing food makes everything taste better.
- If you rush through lunch, you will miss the rhythm that only comes from eating together.
- If you make your own fun, others will join in.
- Sometimes people who bully or cheat need a friend more than a win.
- Not everyone wants to be team captain.
- The weather has no impact on the amount of fun to be had.
- Everyone wants to play; some people just don't know how.
- If you swing too high too fast, the ride is bumpy.

- Sometimes Capture the Flag turns tribal. Remember it is just a game, and it all returns to neutral territory when the bell rings.
- Tag is sometimes a way to touch someone you love, briefly.
- Rules are subjective, and sometimes when you think people are breaking them, they actually play by a different set. Instead of policing, listen, and maybe your game will change for the better.
- The anticipation of recess, while eating lunch, sparks conversation.
- Why walk when you can run?
- It takes courage to include others in your game.
- Everyone makes choices they are not proud of on the playground. The good news is, there is another chance tomorrow to do things differently.
- If you climb up higher than you can jump, you need to be ready to raise the bar.
- There are other alternatives to dividing and conquering besides picking teams.
- Quiet time is productive.
- Your first friend and your first love are hardly ever your last.

Everyone smiles when they say, "Lunch and recess," because they know it's not the answer adults want to hear. Why not? Don't we all feel better when we feel nourished and topped off with chocolate milk, connected with nature and good friends? It is even easier to handle the bullies and the skinned knees, when so much fresh air, fun, and sawdust are swirling.

When I really think about my adult life, I find that many of my successes and failures have been tied to my savvy during lunch meetings and my finesse, or lack thereof, in playground politics. Yes, the math facts and vocabulary come in handy, but real business happens by connecting in powerful ways over lunch while discussing the great game of business.

Maybe our kids are on to something and their answer is not flippant. Perhaps more time at the table, sharing meals, and an abundance of unstructured playtime to figure out who they are, is exactly what they need to succeed now and in the future.

Today I am deliberate about taking a lunch and a recess.

- Carve out time today for lunch or morning tea. It does not have to be at a certain time or a certain place. Just give yourself 30 minutes or more to have lunch and connect in the break room, at the picnic table, or in a café.

- The only rule is you can't multitask with technology. If you mix business with pleasure, it needs to be face to face today. Create a power lunch by simply being present.

Today I am deliberate about taking a lunch and a recess because I recognize the invaluable power inherent in eating and playing well with others.

Venice, Italy

What Contrast Teaches Us About Beauty

In contrast to our honeymoon trip, this visit to Venice was going to be everything the last one wasn't! On our honeymoon it poured down rain, the gondoliers were mostly seeking shelter under bridges, and the lines to see Saint Mark's Cathedral were out the door. There was, however, a magic in the damp air that I could not wait to show our children. This time, I had it planned out, weather and all, and I was ready to show the kids the city Casanova, Marco Polo, and Vivaldi called home.

While Venice was once the center of beauty and elegance in Italy, the Queen of the Adriatic is only a shadow of its former self as it tries to hold on to that image. The graffiti and overflowing garbage cans were only the beginning as we wandered, disillusioned, through the tired *La Serenissima* ("The Most Serene," referring to Venice's title as a republic).

It was not until we left Venice for a jaunt in Innsbruck, Austria, that it became clear to me why Venice fell short. Venice and Innsbruck have virtually nothing in common except for the contrast visiting the two in the same week provided. In Innsbruck, we felt as if we had happened upon life going by in a vibrant city. We watched people meet after work near the river for a tall beer on a checkered table cloth. We played chess in the park with schoolchildren on a field trip, and we wandered into strudel-laden bakeries. We observed ladies tidy the pews at the Cathedral of St. James. Mostly we watched life happening before our eyes.

In Venice, the absence of "real" life happening was palatable. More than 60,000 tourists a day visit Venice, which is more than the number of people who call Venice home. The number of tourists, in such a limited amount of space, forces residents out. It is a strange phenomenon because tourism has been important to Venice for a very long time, but now it is losing the very heart of what makes it such a popular place to visit. It was challenging, during our time there, to find museums open, church doors ajar, and locals to talk to (even for August in Italy) because the cruise-ship industry drives this massive tourism market, and people just come for the day, shop, and leave. The crowds overwhelmed and overshadowed everything and left a very superficial and one-dimensional footprint on a fading gem.

There is a heritage that is being loved, or simply visited to death in Venice. The most frustrating part is that there are glimpses of the beauty and history in the well-worn stones, pocked walls, and intricately carved boats, but we couldn't get to it. We could not wait to leave—not because we didn't want to be there but because what we knew was once there was no longer accessible, and the absence of that authentic Italian character and imperfect glowing allure was sad.

As the hours passed in Innsbruck, and the hikers and bikers descended from the surrounding vertical with animated stories of their adventures, we listened, unnoticed, to the heartbeat of a city in perfect balance.

As Victor Hugo states, "Sublime upon sublime scarcely presents a contrast, and we need a little rest from everything, even the beautiful."

livit

Today I am deliberate in my appreciation of contrast.

- Think of one thing in your life that you would like to be different. It may be your self-image, your marriage, your relationship with a child or a sibling, or your level of job satisfaction. Just identify one area.

- Now say, "Thank you," to that area of your life for being exactly as it is today.

- Contrast will only serve you once you have acknowledged its presence and expressed gratitude for its gifts, whatever they may be.

Today I am deliberate in my appreciation of contrast because I know that without understanding darkness, there is no framework for light.

notes

"And above all, watch with glittering eyes the whole world
around you because the greatest secrets are always
hidden in the most unlikely places. Those who
don't believe in magic will never find it."

– Roald Dahl

Innsbruck, Austria

In the Moment With Mother Nature's Monuments

As mid-July settled over Rome and people from all over the world descended, we knew it was time to go. Our early mornings at the Trevi fountain alone and our lazy evenings listening to music on the Spanish Steps were now ending. Rome was entering its peak season, and it was time to say, *"arrivederci."* We have traversed over diverse landscapes, but the majority of our time has been in mighty, noble cities. We have been voracious students of Western Civilization and its many grand contributions to the world. From Rome to Madrid, to Paris and beyond, we have been humbled, each day, by architectural wonders and artistic genius. Where do we go now to reconnect with each other, away from the crowds, on this popular continent?

As we drove north through the Dolomites and began to explore Tyrol and the Austrian Alps, we knew we had found our place.

The crawling, numerous day-trippers and shoppers were still evident in towns like Merano, Selva di Val Gardena, and Kitzbuhel, but in minutes we could be all alone on an alpine trail, smelling of saccharine hay and dripping berries, with the birds chattering anxiously about our arrival.

As our confidence grew, we wandered deeper into the Zillertal Alps and spent many days alone with some of Mother Nature's monuments. We will never forget the power of the Wasserfalle in Krimml. It is the largest waterfall in Europe and the fifth largest in the world, and it is still dwarfed by the peaks from which it tumbles. The woman collecting mushrooms near the Patscherkofel Peak, who gave us a toothless grin, was the first person we had spotted in three hours and the last we would see on that ominous trail. The storm that draped over the Mayrhofen Valley drove us quickly from the trails back to our cozy rooms over a working dairy in Ellbogen (population 1,000), where we were treated to warm bread and fresh milk each morning.

This region, although not a secret to many, was a hidden, unlikely, glittering place for our family. We discovered magic in the solitude and found the crowds full of joyful noise when we came out of the woods to welcome their company. Up to this point, we have been intent on connecting with culture and history and our ancestry. This time, rooted in the great forests of Tyrol, connected us to each other through the ease and majesty of nature.

Today I deliberately open my eyes to the world around me with intention.

- Make a commitment to look up, out and around.

- What beauty do you find in unexpected places? Is there a flower pushing through the concrete on the sidewalk? Are raindrops caught in a luminous spider's web? Does a puddle reflect a grey sky from a new perspective?

- Simply look for beauty around every corner.

Today I deliberately open my eyes to the world around me with intention because I know that my awareness is a vital part of the magic that reveals itself to me.

notes

*"The only thing worse than being blind
is having sight but no vision."*

– Helen Keller

Bavaria, Germany

Facing Rain on Germany's Romantic Road

As we carefully planned our castle-clad, scenic route along the Romantic Road in Germany, the possibility of rain in August never entered our minds.

As soon as we entered Füssen, fog descended and rain clouds burst and persisted for miles and days on end. After the initial shock of being wedged between hundreds of tour buses, crawling along a crowded, wet road with no visibility, we realized what we were facing.

How can we even expect something aptly named the Romantic Road to ever be that for everyone, every day?

- I expected the children to be mesmerized by the romance and beauty of the German countryside.

- I expected to hold my husband's hand as the car gracefully hugged every turn and the sun beat down on the castles and meadows.

- I expected something very different from what I was experiencing, and I knew I could either take it for what it was or fight the image I had in my mind that was most certainly NOT before me.

We pulled over near the Neuschwanstein Castle (that Disney modeled Sleeping Beauty's Castle after) to get out of the tour-bus traffic that was releasing thousands of people into the umbrella-soaked line reading "3 hours for entry." We knew getting into that line was not what we wanted, but we also knew that it was what we had planned. At what point do we give up the plan and know that the path will reveal itself?

We kept on driving and ended up at Queen Mary's Bridge, where we saw the most beautiful sight imaginable. Neuschwanstein Castle, hovering above the fog, looked as if it were floating in the air. The blanket of dampness blocked all the chaos below, and we were left with just the beauty and majesty of a fairy-tale moment.

As we continued through the Bavarian countryside, the Romantic Road revealed itself in unexpected ways. The kids were glued to their windows, anxious for any form to reveal itself through the mist. The fog lifted just in time for us to see a pack of horses running through a lush, emerald valley. There was just enough light on a black, soupy lake to see a lone white swan gliding under a stone bridge.

The romance of the road came not in its ability to live up to our expectations, but more in its tenuous desire to reveal moments of beauty behind a curtain of mystery. Most of the sites we came here to see were not visible, but because of that, we saw things we never would have otherwise, and with intense clarity.

We were open to meeting the experience for what it was, and it became more than we could ever have planned. It is a lesson we learn over and over again on this journey: The vision is not to see things just as we have imagined them to be. The vision is the freedom to live deliberately every day, and that is something we can do even when it rains on the Romantic Road.

Today I am deliberate in articulating my vision.

Give yourself 5–10 minutes to answer the following questions:

- Why am I here on this Earth at this time?
- Why does it matter than I am on this Earth at this time?
- Why is it important to me to remember why I am here?

Today I am deliberate in articulating my vision because I know that when my vision is clear, it is much easier to make decisions that align with what matters most in my life.

notes

Antwerp, Belgium

When Pulling Up Anchor Is Not a Good Idea

We have been drifting these past two weeks. Why? Because we believed we were too busy to set our anchors in each new place, and we lost our sense of direction. At home, we knew the things that anchored us: family dinner, a walk in the woods, or a fire in the fireplace. Everyone has their anchors or things that ground and orient them wherever they land.

Sometimes we find ourselves in a very foreign place and we forget to drop anchor and orient ourselves. What we need to be doing is the opposite. Anchor first. Then get oriented.

We traveled through four countries on Monday, and we were thoroughly confused by the time we reached our destination near Antwerp, Belgium. We felt that old pull to scatter and find food and banking, but we stopped intentionally to ask, "What are our anchors?" Coffee time and exercise in the morning, walks in the evening, reading before bed, and meals together. We need to focus on these things before we go sightseeing, looking for Wi-Fi, or peeling off in a million directions.

Once we set our anchor as a family, everyone was much calmer heading off to acclimate in his or her own way. The result was that by stopping, we actually grounded ourselves much more quickly and with more ease.

The amazing thing was that the kids started to suggest things that felt grounding to them after our conversation. Our older son wanted to reinstate family movie night. Our younger son wanted to cook one meal a week with me like he did at home. Our daughter wanted to bake on Sundays together. As we steady our sea legs beneath us, what matters most comes to the surface.

Today I am deliberately articulating what anchors me.

- Write down three things that anchor you and make you feel grounded wherever you are. It may be a practice, like yoga, meditation, or a walk in the morning or it might be time with a pet or loved one.

- These are not aspirational anchors or things you hope to start doing. These are things you already know set your course each day, or send you drifting if you don't do them.

- Make sure you do at least one of them today and notice its effect on your productivity.

Today I deliberately articulate what anchors me because I know that the more grounded I feel, the more risks I will be willing to take.

notes

Europe - 13 countries and counting

What Does Citizenship Mean to You?

My husband and kids are officially Italian citizens and have Italian passports in hand. I have been recognized as being married to an Italian citizen, although I had a hunch about that before he had his passport!

My in-laws have never been to Italy, and yet I see them everywhere. The way the ladies at the market move with purpose reminds me so much of my mother-in-law. I see her in the women walking in the *piazza* and how they hold their purses. I see her subtle movements in the many *nonne* I have met cooking in various kitchens across Italy—how their wooden spoon is an extension of their arm and how they know every corner of their kitchen as they dance around obstacles while balancing dishes. I see my father-in-law in so many of the men I have met. I see how he cares for his home as the original do-it-yourselfers do all over Italy. I see his prowess at cribbage and all card games in cafés tucked all over the Old Country.

I see how both of them stop whatever they are doing and take time to talk and connect when someone stops by for coffee. They never seem rushed, although they are very busy and productive citizens. They always make time for family.

Citizenship, I have realized, is about recognizing and documenting a culture that already exists within us. While the papers are proof, the real evidence has come from what we have witnessed this year and who we have been all along.

Culture defies political boundaries. It is carried through generations of immigrants, and it withstands geographical changes. If I had never stepped foot on Italian soil, I don't know if I would have ever understood what it means to be Italian and how much of it is already present in my husband, his family, and our children.

On our next journey we will be exploring my family heritage. We will traverse the verdant cliffs of Ireland and the blustery Scandinavian fall. Will I find people as adept as my Irish grandmother at transforming meat and potatoes into yet another dish? Will I find other old salts in Norway and Sweden who find the smell of fish for breakfast as tantalizing as my father and uncles.

I am so excited to explore aspects of my heritage that I never attributed to culture before now. The Mariotti's are Italian-American, Irish, Scandinavian and a few other things we are off to discover.

Today I am deliberate in living my legacy.

- Think of one thing you can identify as important in your culture.

- Today, tell someone the story of that one thing. Where did your name come from? When was the first time you tasted that cake? Who sang that song for you growing up? Where were you when you heard the story you are telling now for the first time?

- Tell the story today.

Today I am deliberate in living my legacy because I know that when I give my story a voice, it becomes more of who I am.

notes

The journey continues at **www.livology.com**.
See where the Mariotti's are now and sign up to get
great stories 2-3 times a week for free.
They will inspire you wherever you are in your personal journey.

To further embrace the adventure, we also offer **daily livits**
that will be delivered right to your in-box!

Here is what our customers are saying about how
the **daily livits** have enhanced their lives:

*"Such a welcome email in my inbox every day! It's my reminder to
take a deep breath and ponder the wisdom offered of living in the moment ...
The daily Livits help me work toward balance and focus on the most
important details of life as they present themselves. I recommend the
daily Livits to anyone seeking to explore an intentional life."*

- Kathy Matulys

*"I love these. They are absolutely perfect. Sometimes all I have time
to do is read them and it still changes my whole day."*

- Katy Anquetil

Contact us at **www.livology.com** to share your stories and
experiences with us from your corner of the globe.